THE RIVER

The Thames in Our Time

THE RIVER

The Thames in Our Time

PATRICK WRIGHT

THE THAMES

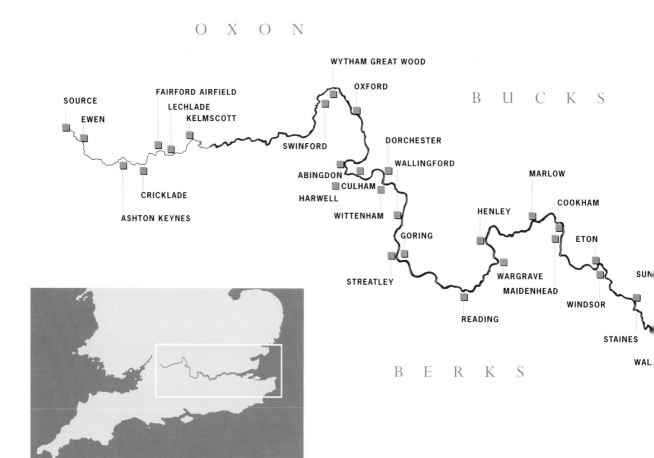

O X O N

WYTHAM GREAT WOOD

OXFORD

B U C K S

FAIRFORD AIRFIELD

SOURCE

LECHLADE

EWEN

KELMSCOTT

DORCHESTER

SWINFORD

WALLINGFORD

MARLOW

ABINGDON

CULHAM

COOKHAM

CRICKLADE

HARWELL

HENLEY

ETON

ASHTON KEYNES

WITTENHAM

SUN

GORING

WARGRAVE

MAIDENHEAD

WINDSOR

STREATLEY

STAINES

READING

WAL

B E R K S

Set in Perpetua and New Gothic
Printed in France by Imprimerie Pollina s.a
Colour separations by Imprimerie Pollina s.a.
Jacket printed by Imprimerie Pollina s.a.

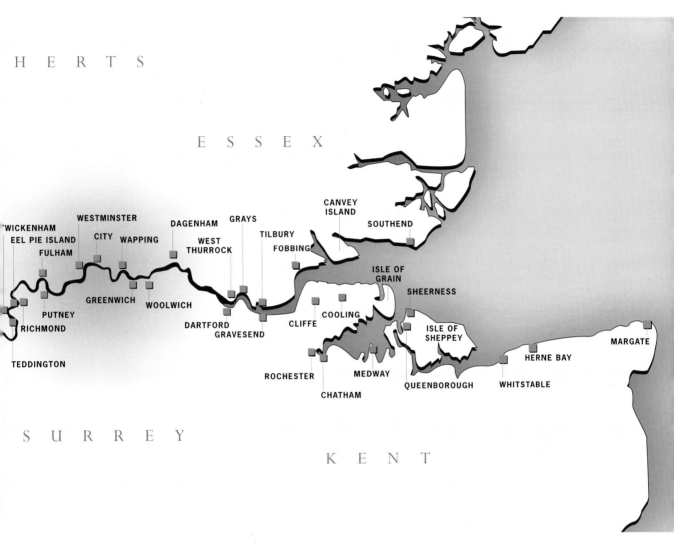

HERTS

ESSEX

CANVEY
ISLAND

WICKENHAM   WESTMINSTER   DAGENHAM   GRAYS   SOUTHEND
EEL PIE ISLAND   CITY   WAPPING   TILBURY
FULHAM   WEST   FOBBING
                        THURROCK
                                                            ISLE OF
                                                            GRAIN
                                                                        SHEERNESS
PUTNEY   GREENWICH   COOLING
RICHMOND   WOOLWICH   ISLE OF
                                                                        SHEPPEY   MARGATE
                        DARTFORD   CLIFFE
TEDDINGTON   GRAVESEND   HERNE BAY

                                                MEDWAY   WHITSTABLE
SURREY   ROCHESTER   QUEENBOROUGH

                        CHATHAM

KENT

Published to accompany the television series *The River*,
first broadcast on BBC 2 in 1999.
Executive producer: Keith Alexander
Series producer: James Runcie
Producers: Nicky Pattison and Adam Low

First published in 1999
© Patrick Wright 1999
The moral right of the author has been asserted.

ISBN 0 563 38478 6

Commissioning editor: Anna Ottewill
Project editor: Martha Caute
Text editor: Barbara Nash
Designer: John Calvert
Picture research: Susannah Parker
Map: Ann Ramsbottom
Specially commissioned photographs: Tino Tedaldi

Published by BBC Worldwide Ltd,
Woodlands, 80 Wood Lane, London W12 0TT

CONTENTS

WHITSTABLE TO ROUGHS TOWER

I first got to know the Thames estuary from the North Kent coast when I was a student in Canterbury in the early seventies. I crossed the Stour to find that the Isle of Thanet was no longer an island: indeed, it had become Margate. At Reculver, where the gaunt twin-towered ruin of St Mary's looms over the water's edge, I ignored the caravans and tried to imagine the ancient settlements lost to the sea here: the once commanding Roman town of Regulbium and also the palace that Ethelbert, the sixth-century Saxon king and Christian convert, is said to have built on its ruins after granting his seat at Canterbury to St Augustine for the establishment of a priory.

I remember Herne Bay as a glacial, eternally out-of-season watering place still geared to extracting money from visitors even though its pier had long since collapsed into the sea. The typical entrepreneur here seemed to run a diversified operation in which holidays and retirement were adroitly interlaced with death. He might start by renting out deck-chairs in the summer, but would soon branch out into servicing the requirements of pensioners foolish enough to spend their last years here. When the sad day finally came, he would probably be there with an undertaking business and, perhaps, also a junk-shop or two to assist with the redistribution of furniture.

A few modest fanfares may have sounded elsewhere when the University of Kent opened in 1965, but in Herne Bay this high-minded initiative only meant an opportunity to rack up the rents for out-of-season flats and rooms. In October, when the commuting students moved in, each of these lucrative nooks was a floral land of grey and pink. By the time the more vengeful students had finished redaubing them in purple and orange and gone off for the long vacation, Herne Bay's summer visitors found themselves returning to rooms that were

Previous pages
Red Sands Army Sea Fort, off Whitstable. This complex of seven towers was built during the Second World War to defend convoys in the Thames estuary. Abandoned after the war, many of these offshore bastions were later recycled as pirate radio stations.

like lurid hallucinations whose rightful owners had just leapt out of the window.

The thought of Herne Bay makes me shudder still, but Whitstable, the town just a few miles west, was always a different matter. I never quite believed locals who proudly insisted that the Romans, having sampled the oysters, quickly decided that they had landed in Paradise. Yet, Whitstable remains an agreeably untidy and multi-dimensional place, with its devil-may-care jumble of shacks and cottages along the sea-wall, its oyster restaurants and Formica whelk and cockle bars, its odd flat-iron building that looks like a forgotten trial-run for Manhattan. There were some famously 'hard' men in this robust, two-fingered town, including 'Pete', a much-rumoured demolition contractor who had removed plenty of war-time debris from the estuary in his time. 'Pete' was the kind of man who would spend a night up in London pouring quick-setting concrete into the drains of a sleeping rival who had crossed him. The next afternoon he could be found sitting in a field gazing contentedly at a single flower or a blade of grass and marvelling at the wonders of creation. Drugs were not just part of 'the student problem' in North Kent at that time.

I never lived in Whitstable, but I came to know it as a supply-teacher at a school that stands on a hillside just above the town, a beleaguered-looking place that gazed out over allotments and jumbled roofs to the Swale estuary, the Isle of Sheppey, and the Thames estuary beyond. Going back to Bellevue Road after twenty-five years, I discovered that the institution I remembered as the Sir William Nottidge Secondary Modern School had recently been taken in hand and relaunched as 'The Community College Whitstable'. A logo reading 'Strive for Excellence' was prominently emblazoned just inside the door, close to a display of newspaper cuttings promising a 'new era' for this famously problematic seat of learning. The new 'House' system was explained in a glossy brochure, as was the new-found importance of parental choice.

It is no easy matter to raise up a secondary modern in a county that still maintains grammar schools, but the new headteacher was adamant that his improvements were not just an exercise in relabelling, and I sincerely hope that time proves him right. When I worked there, years before the age of mission statements and business plans, 'The Nottidge' was a school to which many parents wished, with an ardour that my own presence did nothing to diminish,

they would never have to surrender their children. The fact that I remember my initial interview at all is largely thanks to the four words that were scrawled in prominent letters on the wall of a mobile class-room just outside the main entrance. 'X is a wanker', they said. 'X' was the headteacher of that time and the window in front of which he sat might as well have been the graffiti artist's frame.

Both of us were desperate, so we came to terms soon enough. I started the next morning, a more or less permanent supply-teacher standing in for the regulars as they succumbed to more or less mysterious diseases. 'The Nottidge' cleared me of any desire to pursue a teaching career. There were certainly some dedicated and effective teachers on the staff, but I was not among them; and I had no intention of ending up like their puce-faced colleague whose recurring fantasy was to take Whitstable's incurably delinquent children and isolate each one under an airtight bell-jar.

It was the kids in the back row that he had in mind – wayward characters, some of whom carried the names of pop singers, film stars and even god-like heroes of the ancient world. A number of these recalcitrants were bright as well as unbiddable, and there was something admirably thorough about their deter-mination to make failure their very own.

The Department of Education may have thought otherwise, but for these back-row kids teachers weren't for learning from. They were for practising up your attitudes against, so that you would be well equipped to hold your own in a world full of bosses, bureaucrats, toffs and interfering regulators. One day I was asked to introduce these rough diamonds to the pleasures of poetry. Aware that this was a tall order, I chose the shortest examples I could find, but in a few seconds 'Haiku' had been translated into 'F*** you' and I realized that I could teach them nothing.

They, however, introduced me to a basic fact of estuary life. They taught me that it is not enough to be contemptuous if you are really going to make a go of raising two fingers to the world: you have to be resilient, quick-witted and full of contrary initiative as well. I was happy enough to leave 'The Nottidge' but I remembered those kids in the back row years later, when I heard that the French had started calling English football fans 'Les fuck offs'.

As the French have good reason to know, 'Fuck off' is an ancient English cry, and one that has a venerable tradition along the Thames and its muddy coastal approaches. It's what Boudicca yelled at the Romans as she burned them out of London in AD60. The Ancient Britons shouted it at the Saxons in the fifth century; and by the ninth century, the Saxons were sufficiently Anglicized to be hurling it back at the Vikings shortly before nailing the skins of two lanky Danish raiders to the church door at South Benfleet, Essex. It is, without doubt, an ancient English heritage, far older than warm beer, red pillar boxes and maiden aunts cycling to church. That fact may horrify sensitive souls and depress those – vicars, Marxists and public health inspectors as well as teachers – who have, over the years, tried to bring some redemption to the working class. But you don't have to look far along the Thames estuary to find someone who will raise a couple of fingers at that idea, too.

So, where to begin? Several possibilities lay within the view from Whitstable. The Isle of Sheppey, with its prisons and high incidence of heroin addiction, lies to the west across the estuary of the river Swale – much reduced since the days when it was a navigable route for London-bound ships. When I lived in Kent, the new university's sociologists were busy surveying the previously uncharted extent of England's informal economy in the socialist outpost of Sheppey. Among their scientific findings was the fact that a remarkably high proportion of the Isle's denizens had, at one time or another, rolled up their sleeves and fitted a rolled steel joist into their own houses.

This remains an intriguing discovery, but I was always more fascinated by a large steel structure that could be seen standing far out to sea. From Whitstable, it was little more than a smudge on the ocean horizon, a cluster of tiny grey blobs, like distant wisps of smoke just above the water.

Prevrious pages
**Whitstable, Kent.
A robust two-fingered
town, which the
Romans mistook for
Paradise.**

It was with this mysterious destination in mind that, one day in November, I went to Sheppey and boarded a rusty old tug at Crundel's Wharf in Queenborough. We passed the flat turf of Dead Man's Island, where corpses from the hulks were buried and where coffins are said sometimes still to be exposed by the high spring tides, and we then headed out through the Medway into the open water of the Thames estuary.

The Red Sands Army Sea Fort is one of a series erected during the Second World War, when convoys using the Thames estuary were menaced both by German planes and by E-boats which placed mines in their path by night. Designed by Guy Maunsell, the first four sea forts were built for the Admiralty. Constructed upriver at the Red Lion Wharf at Northfleet, Gravesend, they were then towed out and sunk into their chosen positions on the seabed. Each Admiralty sea fort consisted of a vast pontoon, lozenge-shaped to resist tidal scouring, and two separate towers 24 feet in diameter and 60 feet high. The submerged towers had seven decks for magazines, generators, living and sleeping quarters. The steel superstructure was tiered, with heavy guns on top, Bofors guns below that, and then the officers' quarters, radar and fresh-water storage tanks.

George Hancock was on our boat. A butcher with the Co-op before the war, he had joined the Royal Marines and then served three years among the 'Princes in the tower' on the Admiralty Fort at Sunk Head. Having joined the Fort at Tilbury Docks in the spring of 1942, he followed it out to be sunk in its chosen position; and there he stayed, from late May 1942 until victory in Europe in May 1945. The rota was six weeks on and ten days off, and the men slept in dormitories positioned way down under water inside the old concrete towers. It was, he remembered, an isolated and nerve-wracking existence in which long stretches of boredom were interrupted by moments of intense activity – firing at Doodlebugs and German bombers as they headed up the river, or into the fog as the sound of German voices drifted over from an unseen enemy vessel. On one occasion, a passing American bomber signalled down to Sunk Head fort asking, 'Are you frying tonight?' Having received the answer, 'Yes, please, preferably plaice,' the plane jettisoned its unused bombs into the sea nearby, leaving the marines to take their pick of the stunned fish that floated to the surface.

The scariest moment came one day just after Divisions, as church services were called. The men had just sung 'For those in peril on the sea', when the warning went up that a mine was drifting their way on the tide. They assembled on deck, swimmers sorted from non-swimmers, and waited for the end. George Hancock remembers standing there in the deadly silence, thinking of his family having Sunday lunch at that very moment. He could still hear the clanking of that mine, as it slowly scraped its way past the fort's two concrete towers, before drifting off, still intact, to be detonated by a destroyer.

Red Sands, however, is not an Admiralty fort. As we approached this spooky collection of rusted metal boxes, Mr Hancock explained that it was an army fort of the type built a little later. The intention this time had been to replicate an anti-aircraft gun unit, as might have been established in a field, with generators, anti-aircraft guns and searchlights all placed about 100 feet apart from one another. So Guy Maunsell had come up with a design that included seven separate towers. Each of these consisted of a two-floored steel house mounted on four legs, and the whole complex was linked with light steel bridges that have long since disappeared from Red Sands. As we circled round this clanking relic, George Hancock remarked that boredom had no doubt been a big issue on the army forts, too. Men were encouraged to fend off 'Fort Madness' by engaging

An army sea fort pictured in its original state on 29 September 1945. The design, which was common to all army sea forts installed in the estuary, is based on a field antiaircraft station.

in hobbies – fishing from the fort or making models. It is recorded that, on Shivering Sands Army Fort, 'some really beautiful embroidery and knitting was produced'.[1]

Recycling is an instinctive activity along the Thames estuary – and it can be applied to army forts as well as to scrap metal or to the used fridges that one dealer in Tilbury ships out to be sold in Africa. For a time after the victory of 1945, a care-and-maintenance regime was maintained on both Admiralty and army forts. But it wasn't long before most of these redundant installations were abandoned to the sea. Some were demolished, like the Nore Army Fort, which was removed after being struck by errant ships. In the sixties, however, a number of surviving forts were occupied by rogue males and launched into a curious posthumous existence. Converted into pirate radio stations, they became the offshore bastions of a jangling collusion between the electric guitar and freemarket crusaders bent on defying the dictatorship of the BBC.

It was in this pioneering climate that Michael Bates came of age. A man of various occupations, he is now one of twelve licensed cockle-fishermen working out of Leigh-on-Sea, but he did much of his growing up offshore. He was a young boy when he first visited Knock John army fort. His father, Roy Bates, a Southend-based entrepreneur and former major with the Royal Fusiliers, wanted to see if the fort would be an appropriate place to mount his pirate station Radio Essex ('Britain's Better Music Station'). As Michael recalls, it was on the day that Winston Churchill was buried that he first climbed up a perilous ladder on to this teetering world, filled with dead seagulls and interiors that were 'like going into a cold, dark, dank cave'. They found live ammunition in the generator room, tin helmets hung in rows, a key-rack still bearing labelled keys, and old Senior Service fag-ends for DJs who ran out of smokes. He remembers spending Christmas day on Knock John, but was away at boarding school after that. By the time he made his early departure from that unnamed institution's classrooms, his father had been obliged to fold up Radio Essex and shift to a more remote fort, Roughs Tower, where Michael lived 'for years and years'.

It was the government's legal manoeuvring that forced the move. The early pirate stations had been able to use various coastal forts because they were outside the official three-mile limit. But the 1967 Offshore Broadcasting Act established a new Bay Enclosure Line which was drawn across the mouth of the Thames, and only two of the remaining forts remained outside it: Sunk Head, which the authorities blew up after the pirate operators required an emergency evacuation later that year, and Roughs Tower, the old Admiralty fort which remains Roy Bates's centre of operations to this day.

Having abandoned the place, the British government was considered to be in dereliction of sovereignty so, on 2 September 1967, Bates formally raised his flag on Roughs Tower, declaring it to be 'the Independent Principality of Sealand'. As Michael remembers, 'he made it a principality purely to simplify the legal side of things', and to avoid having to draw up a huge constitution. Instead of establishing an elaborate political regime, he proceeded on the basis that, 'in a principality, the prince's word is law, and that's it'. So Roy Bates, the former pirate, became Prince Roy and his wife, Princess Joan.

To begin with, the British authorities were actively discouraging. Indeed, in October 1968 both 'Roy of Sealand' and his son Michael were in an Essex court, charged with opening fire on an English merchant vessel: they would have claimed self-defence, but the judge ruled that the court had no jurisdiction over Roughs Tower. There has been a stand-off ever since, although the British government remains adamant that while Roy Bates may indeed now be counted as the owner of 'Roughs Tower Gun Platform', his 'principality' lies firmly within British jurisdiction as defined by the Territorial Sea Act of 1987, and therefore has no legitimate existence as an independent state.

Sealand has a flag and its own national anthem. Its coins and stamps may have been produced with an eye on collectors, but driving licences are also said to be available for £100 a piece and many passports have been sold over the years, too. Princess Joan may have come ashore, but Prince Roy and his armed security men are out there to this day, free from bureaucrats and clambering tax inspectors: 'He's chosen to do it. He's seventy-seven now'.

Maunsell's concrete towers are apparently holding up well – 'dry as a bone' right down to the magazine area on the seabed. Yet maintaining tenure has not always been easy. To begin with, as Michael remembers, it was 'a kind of frontier existence' – conducted with candles and hurricane lamps. There are no Indians out in the North Sea, but an independent principality has obvious outlaw attractions, and there were other marauders with an interest in Roughs Tower.

'Some very nasty people came out and had a go at us,' says Michael. 'We eventually came to the conclusion that it was no good just saying "Go away". We had to let them get right underneath and get them in the water so that they didn't come back again. I mean, there were petrol bombs thrown and all sorts of things… The law was not an issue.'

To begin with, the would-be invaders may have been rival pirate radio operators, but, as has happened so often in the history of the estuary, the real heavies came from the Continent. Indeed, on Roughs Tower, the war against Germany and her changing allies seems never quite to have ended. In 1978, Prince Roy went to Salzburg to meet some German and Dutch businessmen with whose help he hoped to convert his principality into an offshore hotel and casino complex. While he was away Sealand was invaded by a helicopter carrying an armed raiding party from the Continent. Recognizing them, Michael Bates allowed them to land, and was promptly tied up and locked in a steel room, where he claims to have been left for three or four days without food or water.

For a while, his captives seemed intent on tossing him into the sea, but eventually a Dutch trawler turned up with the invaders' relief crew, and he was taken off to Holland where he was landed illegally without a passport. He got back to England at about the same time as his father, in time to be informed that ten Belgian ex-paratroopers, equipped with Uzi sub-machine-guns, would soon be landing on Sealand to establish a permanent garrison there.

The Bates' had three days in which to claim their principality back. 'So we went to see a friend of ours who had a helicopter company.' This fellow was a very good pilot – 'he had actually flown in most of the James Bond films'. So they took the doors off the helicopter, and, having practised scaling down ropes at a factory they owned onshore, set off. It was 'quite a fresh day' and just approaching daylight as they came in towards the fort. There was a German fellow in a yellow oilskin, supposedly keeping watch but actually dozing in a chair. Apparently the first thing he saw was a helicopter appearing from underneath the platform, a sight that frightened the life out of him. 'And, as we came down the ropes, they came running out. They were armed.

But we just took them by surprise and wrapped it all up, sort of thing.'

Prince Roy was back in charge of his principality by the time the press arrived the next morning. Drawn to Sealand by rumours of a *coup d'état*, journalists went home to report on Bates's counter-coup, having been shown sawn-off shot-guns and other captured weapons, and also a battered German lawyer, Herr G. Putz, who, as the holder of a 'Sealand' passport, had been convicted of 'Treason' and would remain imprisoned in an ammunition magazine down by the seabed for some forty-nine days.[2] The ultimate estuary outrider, Prince Roy has been in command ever since, presiding over the seagulls and, if the Sealand website is to believed, planning land-reclamation schemes which would provide him with a more permanent and less disputable territory on which to establish his current project, a vaguely defined multi-national and multi-cultural 'Sealand International Business Foundation'.

By 1997 it had emerged that Sealand passports were, in the words of *The Independent*, being 'used by crooks all over the world'.[3] In Hong Kong alone, prior to the Chinese take-over, 4000 Sealand passports were estimated to have

Roughs Tower, an Admiralty sea fort off Felixstowe, which was taken over by 'Prince' Roy Bates in 1967 and renamed the 'Independent Principality of Sealand'.

been sold for £1000 a piece. But it wasn't just that which made them notorious. A Sealand passport was carried by Torsten Reineck, the German on whose houseboat Andrew Cunanan committed suicide after murdering Gianni Versace. Others turned up in Slovenia, where an Austrian couple, one of whom claimed to be Sealand's 'Minister of Economic Affairs', used Sealand passports to open bank accounts into which they funnelled fortunes made from illegal pyramid investment schemes in East Europe. Prince Roy has certainly issued many Sealand passports over the years – the website claims over 160,000 citizens – but he denies all responsibility for any shady dealings by his far-flung citizenry, telling an enquiring reporter that 'The world is awash with fake passports. I'm just angry they're faking mine and using them for illegal purposes.'

'Roy of Sealand' has welcomed diverse visitors to Sealand in his time, including Terry Wogan, but he is more reclusive nowadays. Michael Bates remarks that the place is pretty snug, with three large double-glazed picture windows: 'It's quite spectacular when there's a big storm.' On calmer days, it must be the perfect place to meditate on the 'strange philosophical question' faced by Mr Klaudijo Stroligo, the director of Slovenia's Office for Money Laundering Prevention: 'It was about territoriality and recognition. Did we recognize these passports or not? Who is to say what is or is not a country?'

SHEERNESS: Apocalypse Any Minute Now

Black Deep, Knob Channel, Shivering Sands, the Warp.... The names of the estuary's channels and sands remain suggestive enough, but who nowadays knows about the practical seacraft with which the mariners of earlier generations used to negotiate them? As we sailed back towards the Medway, I found myself trying to remember the inscription on a tombstone in a Canterbury cemetery. This large roughly-hewn monument is engraved with a couplet from the Elizabethan poet Edmund Spenser's *The Faerie Queene*:

> *Sleep after toyle, port after stormie seas*
> *Ease after warre, death after life does greatly please.*

This is a familiar epitaph, but it is especially appropriate in this case, since Jozef Teodor Konrad Korzeniowski, who is buried here, was a Polish-born sea-captain before he was 'Joseph Conrad', the author of *Lord Jim*, *Victory*, *Nostromo* and other sea-faring novels: a man, in other words, who really understood what it was to reach 'port after stormie seas'.

Many Thames' chroniclers start at the source, preferring the swanny upstream shires to London and the tidal river. But Joseph Conrad, whose description is entitled 'The Faithful River', approaches from the opposite direction. Indeed, his Thames is entirely confined to the estuary as it once led up to the London docks. Published in 1906 as part of *The Mirror of the Sea*, 'The Faithful River' is shaped by working knowledge of the estuary, its shifting sands, currents and winds. Yet its author also enjoys an exotic turn of phrase. Looking at the gaps and alleys that reach down on to the foreshore through the densely clustered warehouses along the London riverside, Conrad thinks of 'the paths of smashed bushes and crumbled earth where big game comes to drink on the banks of tropical streams'. He likens the domed storage tanks of an oil refinery clustered near the water's edge to the huts of a Central African village. He spies the most dismal concrete factory near the Essex town of Grays, and declares it as characteristic of the Thames estuary as a palm grove on a remote coral strand.

Conrad's literary flourishes were far-fetched in a curiously literal sense. The Thames that he knew in the late nineteenth century was an imperial river, a 'waterway leading to the uttermost ends of the earth', as he described it in *Heart of Darkness*, and Conrad had himself sailed its distant reaches. In his book, every odd figure of speech is grown from an exotic fruit gathered at the edges of empire, repatriated, and then planted along the Thames estuary at the moment of arrival.

It was Conrad's always offshore view that 'the estuaries of rivers appeal strongly to an adventurous imagination'. Yet he knew that 'their appeal is not always a charm'. Mudflats, after all, are austere and grim-looking places, and low sand-banks are not always improved by their 'shabby and scanty vegetation'. And yet Conrad insisted that the 'dispiriting ugliness' of an estuary was sometimes only a 'repulsive mask', and rarely more so than on the Thames which was less built-up and therefore more open to 'romance' than any other commercial English river.

The estuary shore is littered with relics of the imperial history that Conrad knew, and of a long-running drama of invasion and defence that extended up through the Second World War. But nowadays this history seems strangely disconnected from the present. Indeed, in our time, the romance of the estuary lies in the experience of coming across your own history and realizing, whether with sadness, bewilderment or an unexpected sense of relief, that it consists so largely of voids, hulks and ruins.

Much of the debris scattered around the estuary is inert, but this is not a place where history is entirely without potency in the present. Just south of Nore Sand, where the river Medway flows into the Thames, we passed the tilted and protruding mastheads of the *USS Richard Montgomery*, a sunken American munitions ship packed with bombs and drums of phosphorus which has lain here since 20 August 1944. Ordered to anchor in the wrong place as a result of an error in Southend harbour, this 'Liberty' ship got worked into the sand-bank by a spring tide, and its hull broke before retrieval was possible. Judged too dangerous to move even half a century later, the *Richard Montgomery* is a well-known local feature, lurking offshore in its buoyed-off 'Danger Area' and reputedly still capable of obliterating the nearby town of Sheerness on the Isle of Sheppey.

In the late seventies, this 'time bomb' was turned into a symbol of 'the spiritual situation of the age' by Uwe Johnson, one of the greatest German novelists of the post-war period.[4] An East German who escaped to the West in 1959, Johnson's career had not been short of prizes and prestigious visiting appointments at Harvard and other American universities. Yet he chose to live in Sheerness, where he went by the name of 'Charles' and could be found most evenings in one of the nearby bars. The elderly cellarman at the Napier Hotel in Alma Road remembers Johnson as 'a nice fellow' who drank strong lager, chain-smoked French cigarettes, and always had a book with him. Johnson's sympathies were well to the left of the political spectrum and, having removed himself from both Germanys, East and West, he lived for ten years in what is sometimes still called 'the people's republic of Sheppey': anonymous, if not exactly reclusive, and distanced from his own unwanted reputation as the novelist of divided Germany. It's an odd thought, as the critic Greg Bond observes, that the 'Charlie' who could be seen walking over to a greasy Sheerness snack bar for breakfast was actually one of the most high-powered German intellectuals of the age.

Entitled 'An Unfathomable Ship', Johnson's essay about the *Richard Montgomery* takes the side of the people of Sheppey against the history (and also the successive British governments) that obliged them to live with the prospect of fiery inundation hanging over their heads. On first arriving in Sheerness in 1974, Johnson may well have shared the misperception of the visitors who, so he suggests, might easily mistake the 'slanting stakes' sticking out of the water for eel traps. But the locals delighted in disabusing visitors of this error. 'However dark the cloud, it still has a silver lining,' they said, adding that in Sheerness, much of which is below sea level, the cloud was the sea that had flooded the town in February 1953, and which would return sporadically to do the same until the present sea-wall was built. As for the silver lining, that was the *Richard Montgomery*. Known as 'our wreck' and 'the Grand old Lady of the Thames', it was also 'our only spectacle'.

The *Richard Montgomery*, an American Liberty ship which sank off Sheerness in 1944, laden with bombs. Too dangerous to move, it remains there to this day, a fiery inundation waiting to happen.

If this 'unfathomable' ship blew up, which even the responsible authorities admitted was possible, it would surely devastate Sheerness and cause serious damage as far away as Sittingbourne. It would engulf the Isle of Grain with its oil refinery directly across the Medway from Sheerness; and it might also, so local speculation claimed, strike a passing oil super-tanker with a fireball, initiating a chain reaction that could ignite the even greater quantities of oil and methane gas stored on the Essex shore around Canvey Island. As for the tidal wave likely to follow any explosion, that would pour up the Thames towards London – although, as Johnson noted drily, 'the Houses of Parliament and Whitehall were unlikely to be affected'. In the meantime, the American hulk sat there, visible from Johnson's house on Marine Parade, its cargo of more than 3000 tons of bombs left uninspected since 1952.

People around Sheerness were accustomed to counting up the ways the *Richard Montgomery* might be detonated: accidental impact with a passing ship (Johnson claimed that twenty-four near-collisions had already been logged at the local coast-guard station); bombs falling on one another as intermediate decks collapsed; pressure waves from a low-flying jets. It might be set off deliberately by students (some of whom had threatened to do just that during their 'rag week' of 1969), by an obstinate philologist determined to test the saying that 'whoever sets the Thames on fire will perform miracles', or by a suicide 'afraid of being lonely'.

Johnson himself died in March 1984, struck down by a heart-attack at forty-nine years old, and for two weeks his body lay unfound in his English retreat. His article on the *Richard Montgomery* may be well-regarded in Germany, but it should be better known here too: a Thames allegory in which history is treated not in the upriver style as a tranquil and reassuring stream of national destiny – but as a submerged and unstable charge that still has the power to blow up in our faces.

KARAOKE IN GRAIN

There is an eeriness as well as a defiantly posthumous vitality that clings to remote Kentish places like the Isle of Grain. Even without knowledge of the nearby *Richard Montgomery*, to walk in the shadow of Grain power station is to preview the end of the world. Behind the sea-wall lies a splendidly bleak expanse of marsh, littered with relics of industry and war. Signs warn of danger and sur-veillance, electronic or otherwise. Accustomed to living among these gaunt ruins, various locals have added old beds, sofas and fridges to the scene; and the conservationists have been through, too – grafting their concern for wildlife and ecology on to the dereliction. Less an imperial landscape than a redundant and forgotten one, Grain speaks of abandonment on a grand scale.

A few hundred metres inland, I found a settlement of red-brick houses with a few modest amenities. There's an old Bethel Congregational Chapel and also 'Ozzie's Plaice', trading in fish and chips, burgers and kebabs. An unprepos-sessing brick bunker doubles as 'Joe's Cabaret Bar' and 'Ed's Diner'. I watched it come into its own on karaoke night. The bouncer provided beefy support for the owner Shirley Thomas's insistence that she wasn't going to tolerate the troubles associated with a rival drinking establishment somewhere even further into the night. The singing was spirited – particularly that of an arm-whirling lady called Elaine who belted out an uproarious imitation of Kate Bush's 'Wuthering Heights'. This was England, at least as far as one American seaman was concerned. A great bearded fellow who looked like a Mormon prophet, this Texan had just emerged, blinking, from the bowels of a container ship and would be sailing from Grain, almost certainly still blinking, in the morning.

The sign identified Ed's Diner as 'the island venue worth travelling to', but some prospective visitors may be relieved to hear that there is also a more con-ventional, ancient-looking country pub in Grain, an incongruous relic called The Hogarth Inn. I was surprised to come across the name of one of the greatest and, indeed, most assertively English of English artists in this bleak and little-visited place. Stepping inside I was assured that Hogarth had actually stayed there: the news was delivered emphatically, as if he had only stepped out a few minutes before.

On reflection, it seems appropriate that Grain should have found its place on this unconventional early eighteenth-century tourist's itinerary. Hogarth has been called 'the first English-born master of pictorial art', but he was also a great champion of home-grown arts and of the unprettified native landscape. He came here on his famous 'peregrination' of 1732, by which time he was already embarked on a more or less lifelong assault against the connoisseurs and foppish aristocrats who cultivated a modish taste for foreign art, while neglecting native geniuses like Shakespeare and, indeed, Hogarth himself.[5]

Having resolved to undertake their peregrination while drinking in Covent Garden, Hogarth and his three friends sailed to Gravesend and then proceeded to Rochester, before making their disorderly way up the Medway towards Grain. In one 'sharp engagement' it was recorded that 'Tothall and Scott both Suffer'd by their Cloaths being Daub'd with Soft, Cow Dung'.[6] On the way, they stopped at Hoo Churchyard, where Hogarth paid unconventional tribute to a well-born gentleman buried there. Their record recalls

> Hogarth having a Motion; untruss'd upon a Grave Rail in an unseemly Manner which Tothall Perceiving administred penance to ye part offending with a Bunch of Netles. This occasion'd an Engagement which Ended happily without Bloodshed and Hogarth Finish'd his Business against the Church Door.

William Hogarth's portrayal of his own departure from the Isle of Grain in 1732.

Overleaf **Grain Tower at low tide.**

Grain was a notorious smugglers' resort in those days; and The Hogarth Inn, then known as the 'Chequer Alehouse', was kept by a certain Goody Hubbard, who amply entertained her visitors with 'Salt Pork, Black Bread, Butter and Bunns and Good Malt Liquor'. Even so, one night in Grain was quite enough for these uproarious peregrinators. They packed up in the morning, but found it quite difficult to get off the island. The ferryman who would normally have rowed them across the Medway to Sheerness 'did not care to go', and their chosen substitute also declined, saying that 'the wind blew too hard'. In the end, they were advised to make their way across the marsh to the salt-houses near the point, and to stand there in the hope of hailing a passing boat. By this means, and for a fee of two shillings and ten pence, did one of England's greatest artists escape from the Isle of Grain, although not before enduring the difficult embarkation duly recorded in the fifth of his peregrinatory illustrations.

MARSH FEVER IN HOO

If Hogarth and his friends hastened away, this was partly because of the insects that flourished in this muddy stretch of Kent. They had slept badly the night before arriving in Grain: 'At three awaked and Cursed our day; our Eyes Lipps and Hands being Tormented and Swell'd by the biting of gnats.'

I remembered those words as I stood before the graves of Michael and Jane Comport in the redundant churchyard of Cooling, a remote inland village on the Hoo Peninsula a few miles to the west of Grain. The Comports were a considerable eighteenth-century couple who lived just down the road at Cooling Castle. Thought originally to have stood on the Thames but now stranded two and a half miles inland, this moated bastion was built in the 1380s, not long after the French sacked Gravesend. It had been the home of Henry VI's military commander Sir John Oldcastle, a follower of Wycliffe and champion of the English Bible, who is sometimes said to have been the inspiration for Shakespeare's Falstaff.

Oldcastle was executed for his heresies in 1417, but the Isle of Hoo was to prove dangerous ground for the Comports, too, as their graves make clear. There is nothing exceptional about the adult headstones, but beneath them is arrayed a terrible legion of dead babies, each one marked by a small, sad lozenge of grey stone: thirteen lost infants in all, the Comports' own and others added later by relations who suffered the same affliction. The sight was apparently too much for Charles Dickens, who opened his novel *Great Expectations* in this bleak, abandoned place. He had reduced the stone lozenges to five by the time he imagined Magwitch, his escaped convict from the hulks, rising up at Pip from among the overgrown gravestones.

The ancient fatality of the North Kent marshes still speaks through those stones, although by the Comports' time the killers were not French or Dutch invaders nor even the corrupt establishment of the Church. Indeed, they were altogether closer to the 'gnats' that had worried Hogarth and his fellows fifty years previously. The 'marsh fever' that carried off the Comports' babies was almost certainly malaria borne by mosquitoes of the *Anopheles atroparvus* species.

The last significant outbreak of indigenous malaria on the Isle of Grain occurred in 1918, when English mosquitoes are thought to have picked up the malaria parasite from soldiers returning from Greece and India. In earlier centuries, however, the marshes on both sides of the Thames estuary were fatal places to live. Their mortality rate was well above the national average, and many parishes conducted considerably more burials than baptisms – a dismal condition that historians of disease name 'burial excess'.[7] The dangers of marshland life were recognized long before marsh fever, or the 'ague' as it was also called, was understood except as what one sixteenth-century observer called 'a certain spirituous miasma' associated with 'vapours' from stagnant water. An eighteenth-century historian described the marsh dwellers as being of a 'dingy yellow colour' thanks to their distempers, and recorded that 'it is not unusual to see a poor man, his wife, and whole family of five or six children hovering over their fire in their hovel, shaking with an ague all at the same time'. Observers reported that many marsh-dwelling children were pot-bellied due to their enlarged spleens, known as 'ague-cakes'. Opium-eating babies were recorded too – 'wasted' and 'wizened like monkeys'.

Marsh fever introduced a defining 'contour of death' into the estuary landscape, and one that appears to have been recognized in the sixteenth century when a certain Lambarde claimed that the name 'Hoo' was taken from the Old

English 'Hoh' meaning 'Sorrowe or Sickness'.[8] People who were in any position to avoid living below this contour stayed on the uplands, safe in the knowledge that even the slightest elevation could make all the difference. Educated people kept away. Vicars assigned to marsh parishes proved highly reluctant to take up residence among their parishioners, and landowners knew better than to live on their fertile marshland acres. (It is said that the Comports were 'about the last wealthy family' to remain in the Hundred of Hoo). The marshes were left to a desperate population who were hardly in any position to care whether they lived or died – convicts, smugglers and 'lookers' who farmed these dangerous wastes for absentee owners.

The malaria has gone along with the convict hulks, but Dickensian fogs still roll over the Hoo peninsula and strange residues cover this once fatal land, as I found on the marshes north of Cliffe. If this remote village can still boast a vicar nowadays, it seems unlikely that he or she would repeat the complaint of a pre-decessor who recorded that 'the poor do not attend Church from the use of spirituous liquors which the bad air seems to render necessary as a protection from agues'. The developers are advancing, but one can still sense the otherness of the marshes that stretch out to the north of this village with its old medieval shoreline. The rough track leads past flooded clay pits, an isolated metal barn, part of which seems to have been converted into a house, and on into a fen-like wilderness that stretches out under a vast leaden sky. The map identifies this forgotten place as 'The Poplars', but it feels more like Siberia.

Ornithologists, wildfowlers, and trail-bikers may occasionally pass through, but the only man I met here was Keith Loveridge, a sheep farmer, and I followed him as he rounded up his flock. We walked past strange mounds of earth and stepped over the disintegrating platforms of vanished buildings. The remnants of a narrow gauge railway broke through the grass in places, and the pillars of an overhead hoist stretched away, broken and haywire, towards a jetty that no longer existed beyond the sea-wall.

It's not just the hoop ear-ring and the tinted glasses that set Keith Loveridge apart from the kind of farmer who is born to ancestral acres and a lifetime's worth of Euro-subsidized Range Rovers. His farm is an improvisation laid over the unmarked ruins of a massive explosives factory that once employed many

Opposite **The graves of the Comport family in Cooling churchyard. The thirteen infants died of marsh fever.**

hundreds of workers. Founded in 1901, Curtis and Harvey's factory was soon being described as 'the largest and most completely equipped explosives factory in the kingdom'. It thrived through the First World War and was eventually closed in 1922, a casualty of the Nobel Group's 'rationalization' of the British industry. Fatal accidents were not infrequent, despite the precautionary earth walls or 'hills' that were raised up around the timber buildings in order to direct accidental blasts upwards. Some nitro-glycerine and cordite paste went up one scorching day in July 1911: reducing timber huts to craters, more or less vaporizing three men, and greatly increasing absenteeism the following morning.[9]

As for Keith Loveridge, only a few years ago he was selling used cars in Northfleet, Essex. But he got tired of the red tape, and the increasing difficulty of making a decent living by recycling motorized metal boxes. So, he sold his business and scraped together just about enough to relaunch himself as a sub-sistence farmer. He's chosen a hard life but admits to no regrets at all. Indeed, he loves it out here, especially in the remoteness of winter, and thrives on the isolation. So do his wife and four children, who, as he remarks with evident satisfaction, now find the real world more interesting than TV. Keith Loveridge smiled just a little triumphantly as we parted. I remembered the Sir William Nottidge School in Whitstable, and, rightly or wrongly, chalked up another victory for the back row.

DEATH AND LIFE IN GRAVESEND

Fifty years ago, the novelist and essayist Richard Church, who was then writing a guide to the county of Kent, stepped on to Gravesend High Street from Tilbury Ferry and felt as if he was entering a foreign country. The innumerable shop signs hanging out over the street seemed 'like those in a Chinese city'. There were many 'eating houses', albeit 'rather of the forecastle than the quarter-deck kind' and he appreciated 'a certain robust hornpipe quality about its people. One expects to see a parrot in every front room, and a tattooist's shop round every corner.'[10]

A Blue Amazon parrot called Captain Morgan may sometimes still be encountered at J. & R. Starbuck, the chandlers around the corner in West Street. Yet when I passed through, Gravesend's High Street was an empty thoroughfare: a blighted street-shaped void on which commerce seemed only to stagger, moribund, down the hill towards a river which, sadly, was already lined with corpses.

The council was trying to reverse this depressing tendency by restoring defunct buildings in accordance with its 'Strategy for Action Plan', and promising to relaunch Gravesend's forsaken High Street as a new 'Heritage Quarter'. A free house called The Three Daws seemed already to have made the conversion, so the last refuge available to that old 'hornpipe' quality was a 'Continental' barber's shop, holding out among the boarded-up buildings.

When the new age finally dawns 'Tom' the barber will have little trouble converting his 'Yea old' into the more conventional 'Ye Olde', but he will have to take more radical action about the hairstyles still honoured in his shop. Farewell, surely, to the Boston and the teddy-boy quiff. His walls may be covered with nostalgic pictures of liners and boats, but Tom, whose irregular opening hours reflect both urban blight and the fact that he is himself largely retired, is in little doubt that the Thames has had its day, too. Ask him about the council's plans for an afterlife, and he remarks that, like everything the council promises, he will believe it when he sees it. It's one thing for the council to conjure up 'heritage' against the town-killing trends of recent history, but the missing spirit of commerce is more likely to reappear in the Bluewater shopping centre, a massive and emphatically 'out of town' new development west of Gravesend. Described by its architect as 'the most powerful retail engine built at any one time in Europe', Bluewater is destined to be Kent's answer to Essex's 'Lakeside' on the north shore. In the way of such things, it will also make both Dartford and Gravesend sprawl.

No longer used by the Tilbury ferry, Gravesend's Town Pier is a terminal end-stop at the very bottom of the High Street. The mural at its entrance shows the Watermen's Riot of 22 June 1833. The Gravesend watermen were an indigenous brotherhood who made their living by ferrying people between ship and shore. Their rates were often said to be extortionate, and they were not impressed when Parliament took steps to enable a Town Pier to be built in Gravesend. The

mural shows these heroic brothers hacking at and setting fire to the temporary pier that was already in operation, while red-coated soldiers struggle to prevent them.

Time has since done much of the work those watermen intended. Though somewhat lifted by its mural, the oldest cast-iron pier in the world is promptly depressed again by a wooden canopy which leaves it resembling the back entrance to a redundant railway station. A tweed-jacketed architect who pulled up just as I was inspecting it told me that this 170-year-old pier had been engineered by the man whose bridge joined Buda to Pest in Hungary.

A hundred years ago, excursionists could pay a penny at the Town Pier's entrance, and then walk in to find an amenity that combined 'the business of a steamboat-pier and landing-stage, with a somewhat feeble effort in the direction of bazaar keeping'.[11] The penny is not required nowadays. Step inside, past a discouraging assortment of 'Private' notices, and you find yourself walking along a deserted corridor with greasy, B&B-style carpet underfoot.

If mould can exercise a pincer movement anywhere, it is certainly doing it on the walls of Gravesend's Town Pier, creeping in from both ceiling and floor to encircle the remaining patches of dryness. Further out over the river, the distressed corridor gives up altogether and collapses into a dead restaurant. There's a dance floor and a series of sub-Hogarthian prints of eighteenth-century life set into panels in the wall-paper. The giant stone ash-tray turns out to be a defunct 'water feature', which once burbled away among the shrimp cocktails.

I was surprised to find Michael Cheeseman sitting in an office at the end of this incongruous ruin. His company, C. Crawley Ltd, own the pier, and also seven rusty tank barges, two of which are tied up outside his window at the end of the pier. A family business which thrived in the thirties, Crawley Ltd still ships oil about the estuary for Shell and BP. Recent years may have seen increased trade in the containerized world of the Port of London Authority, but the PLA's glossy brochures haven't made much of an impression here. The word on Gravesend's Town Pier, is that the working river is dying: 'Dead… busted … never get it back.'

Michael Cheeseman has heard rumours about the coming new world in which 'loft-living', leisure, and Richard Branson promise to achieve such

Opposite
Looking north from Gravesend's beleaguered High Street. The Town Pier no longer serves shrimp cocktails.

miracles of regeneration. Shaking his head with ironic amazement, he admits that he had recently been up to London for a conference about the Thames and what it might become in the dawning age of the Millennium Dome. He had felt increasingly itchy as he heard dreamy speakers, who obviously had no practical knowledge of the river, describe it as a 'cultural resource' and a 'united theme' that was 'all of a piece' from source to mouth.

Once they had finished making liquid history of the muddy waters that Cheeseman knows so well, these visionaries had turned their attention to the estuary's ships, conjuring away unsightly rustbuckets like Mr Cheeseman's oil barges and replacing them with sleek, high-speed 'riverbuses' which would somehow manage to abolish time and space, to say nothing of the tides, fog and rain.

Scepticism was plainly in order; and yet, such is the decline of the old working river that Michael Cheeseman was himself already reaching out for the afterlife that has been tried and tested in London's Docklands. Encouraged by a repairs notice served by the council, he had felt obliged to come to terms with this implausible new climate in which even the most decayed and redundant of the estuary's old fixtures was apparently to be lifted with mission statements, marketing rhetoric and 'vision'.

So, like others all over the estuary, Mr Cheeseman, too, eventually pulls out an architect's drawing showing his derelict property transformed. No debris left over from a horrible old restaurant; no more greasy carpets, oil barrels or yellowed plastic windows. Instead here is the Town Pier as a gleaming 'destination' – a crystal palace of steel and glass full of happy people taking their pick of the wine bars, pizzerias, and probably even the bagel counters, too. Cheeseman's scheme was a million or two pounds short of reality, but he was getting the council on his side. A few weeks later, the plans would be on the front page of the local newspaper, with Michael Cheeseman saying, 'We are very positive that the pier will become an asset to the community of Gravesend'.[12]

A less neglected Gravesend asset is buried not far away from the Town Pier, beneath the parish church of St George. Princess Pocahontas was the converted Christian daughter of the Powhatan Indian leader Wahunsonacock. Having married an English pioneer, she visited England in 1617, a time when the original 'Jamestown' colony was only ten years old and still dependent on Indian corn for its survival. She had an audience with James I, but died while anchored at Gravesend having fallen ill while waiting for the wind that would take her back to Virginia.

This accident has since been turned into Gravesend's most picturesque historical anecdote. The parish church in which Pocahontas was buried was long ago replaced by another, itself now venerable enough to prompt the usual anxieties about the cost of conservation. But a statue of Gravesend's Indian princess presides over St George's churchyard: adorned with feathers, Pocahontas looks disconcertingly Disney-like as she gazes out over car parks and the shopping centre.

There is true sadness in Pocahontas's story, not least because her journey hints at the different relationship that might have developed between English colonists and native Americans. But I couldn't detect much sense of this in Gravesend's feathery statue. Indeed, the monument seemed to portray immigration as an exotic and freakish misfortune, a disconnected accident of history that was unlikely ever to happen again.

Gravesend remembers Pocahontas, but what about the 'Lascars' (sailors from the East Indies) who once died here in the most abject of circumstances? It is said that by 1914, 17.5 per cent of the seamen working on British-registered ships were natives of the Indian subcontinent.[13] Originally, these 'Lascars' may have been confined to ships working the Indian Ocean but, by 1782, East India Company officials were writing to Madras complaining that Lascars were calling at their London office 'reduced to great distress and applying to us for relief'. Rules were introduced in an attempt to govern recruitment, maintenance aboard, and repatriation after voyages; and the East India Company was made responsible for housing Lascars during their stay in London. In 1795, a boarding house was opened in Kingsland Road, near Shoreditch in East London; and, at the close of the Napoleonic war, a barracks at Gravesend was dedicated to the accommodation of these stranded unfortunates. Conditions at these places were such that a number of concerned men formed a committee, with residents of Mile End, Shoreditch and

Hackney prominent in its membership. On 9 December 1814, a 'memorial concerning the Asiatic sailors' was printed in *The Times*, alongside the committee's appeal for donations.

This 'memorial' reported that Lascars often became sailors after being 'forcibly taken from the street' in India. Many were placed on ship by Asian intermediaries called *ghat serangs*, who would go on to extract money from their meagre wages. The Lascars might be offered 'animal food' while going on board, but, once the voyage was underway, they were unlikely to receive anything but a small ration of rice and perhaps some ghee. Clothing, if provided at all, was inadequate, and there was often no medical attendant. Meanwhile, ship owners frequently refused to pay even the negligible wages agreed.

Once disembarked in London, Lascars could quickly find themselves in desperate straits. The missionary committee may have described its own anxieties when it noted that the Lascars' health was sometimes threatened by 'promiscuous intercourse with the most abandoned females', but there were more pressing dangers than that. Lascars had been found wandering the winter streets in 'a state bordering on absolute nudity'; and it was said that attendants at the barracks to which the East India Company referred them often tore up their papers of assignment, and left them to freeze like dogs.

Opposite **Asian sailors, or 'Lascars', attending the opening of the Tower Hill memorial to lost merchant seamen in London, December 1928.**

Things were apparently not much better for those who did manage to gain admittance. They were found to be sleeping on 'bare and damp boards' in unheated rooms. No attempt was made to segregate the sick from the healthy, and, during cold months, it was customary for six, eight, or ten Lascars to be found dead in the morning. Meanwhile, there was the 'too general practice with the superintendent and his assistants of capriciously beating the Lascars; and of withholding the whole or part of their food from them'.

Other 'inhuman and excessive' punishments were said to be carried out by Lascars on their own number. Combining against one another, they would reputedly rope their victims' wrists and then suspend them, with toes barely touching the ground, from ceiling beams in their lodging room. It was claimed that they would also tie their fellows to the pump in the yard, perhaps in batches of ten, and then beat them 'with a cane for a considerable time on their bare bodies out of the view of the public'. The committee objected that this behaviour was 'not in unison with the wise and humane laws of England' and, indeed, that the condition of the Lascars in London should be 'reprobated by every humane and liberal mind'. As a result of such agitations, a parliamentary committee was formed to investigate the plight of 'Lascars and other Asiatic Seamen'. On visiting the East India Company's Lascar barracks at Gravesend, its members confirmed the suspicions of the missionary societies: the place was unheated and the Lascars were left to lie, or die, on bare boards, without blankets, furniture or hammocks.

I could find no knowledge of the East India Company's Lascar Barracks in Gravesend today – only the assurance that, wherever such an institution might have stood, it will long since have been demolished.

However, my enquiries at the reference library did turn up something that sent me back to Gravesend's churchyard, with its statue of Pocahontas. There was never the remotest chance that this Kentish town would be colonized by Powhatan Indians, and yet, one day in the early 1960s, the vicar of St George's stepped out of his church and observed that an 'Indian township' had indeed sprung up on his doorstep.

Its occupants were Sikh immigrants from the Punjab, and the vicar, Canon

Selwyn Gummer, was so concerned by their arrival in Gravesend that he teamed up with his son, John Selwyn Gummer, now remembered as the Conservative Minister of Agriculture who tried to bluff his way through the BSE crisis, and the two of them wrote a book entitled *When the Coloured People Come*.[14]

Published in 1966, this work set out to tell the story of '3500 Sikhs, building their lives in an English town', and to assess 'the problems their coming has created against the background of national political action'. Convinced that employment statistics could not be the main measure of integration, the Gummers addressed themselves to 'the kind of lives the newcomers lead', and the difficulties that their culture posed for the host community. It was feared that British cities might flare into Chicago-style violence unless they learned the lessons of Gravesend, which the Gummers deemed to have been successful despite continuing friction.

Having landed at Tilbury, the newcomers had crossed the Thames to Gravesend, where their settlement is said to have been assisted by a shadowy sponsor, perceived to move up and down the river with an uncanny ease reminiscent of Sax Rohmer's Chinese 'devil doctor' Fu Manchu: 'at one time in the early days a mysterious and expensive yacht was to be seen anchored at various points on the Thames…it belonged to a wealthy Asian who was engaged in financing the mass settlement of his fellow-countrymen in Gravesend'. With or without this fellow's assistance, the newcomers were soon packed into the run-down houses that, in those days, still crowded around St George's in the 'chaotic disorder' recorded by Conrad at the beginning of the century.

Tensions emerged as Gravesend awoke to the presence of this 'closed community' in its midst. Natives were wary of the smell of unfamiliar spices, noise and overcrowding (the Gummers report that twenty-four men were living in one small cottage). There was a difficult incident in 1959, when a white tenant who had been quite within his rights under British law to withhold rent due to his Sikh landlord is said to have been roughed up on the basis that 'Mr Ball, you pay not rent'. The present-day reader might notice a certain anthropological loftiness about some of their observations, but the Gummers' conviction that 'a tolerant society will not inevitably lead to integration' was not based on hatred, and there were none of Enoch Powell's foaming 'rivers of blood' in their rhetoric. As they saw it, there was a job of work to be done if violence was to be avoided. St George's had consequently formed a 'mission to the Sikhs', and the Gummers heaped much praise upon the name of Pran Nanda, the man who had taken on the job.

The narrow streets that housed Gravesend's first Sikh settlement have long

since been demolished. The 'closed community' that worried the Gummers has gone, and Gravesend is unmistakably a mixed town. The visitors of earlier generations might have counted up the prodigious number of pubs in Gravesend, or the many pilots and sea-captains who lived in the town. But to walk around the place now is to see more turbans than salty dogs and parrots. According to the Social Services Department, 10 per cent of Gravesend's 93,000 people originate from Minority Ethnic Communities, and the great majority of that number are Punjabi Sikhs.

According to Shaminder Bedi, who works at the Guru Nanak Day Centre for

Gravesend '99 – getting by without parrots or salty dogs.

Gravesend's Ethnic Elderly, the first settlers were men who came into a world of industrial jobs – at paper mills, building sites, and the Bata shoe factory across the river in Essex. Many came in response to advertisements placed in the Punjabi newspapers by a British government keen to attract workers. Others, including Bedi's father, came on a voucher provided after his military service.

I asked whether Gravesend was still defined by the opportunities presented by the river. 'Sadly not', thought Bedi. The population certainly reflected Britain's imperial history, but the Thames no longer sustained or defined the possibilities of the town. The old river-based industries had died and been replaced, if at all, by the usual collection of supermarkets and shopping centres. These changes were regrettable in one sense, and yet the Asians had also thrived as they found 'other ways of making a living rather than just depending on the river'.

As for the 'closed community' described by the Gummers, the Sikh community may indeed have stuck together in the early days, feeling safety in numbers and assuming, anyway, that once they had made some money they would go back to Punjab and buy a few extra fields. But priorities changed once the families arrived. As they came to feel at ease, these industrious newcomers spread out and there is now hardly an area of Gravesend where they have not settled. The first generation may have laboured in factories, farms and building sites, but a considerable number of their children have gone on to become accountants, solicitors, doctors and dentists. Lots of Gravesend Sikhs now have their own businesses, and not just corner shops either. When it comes to 'integration', there are networks which make it possible to solve problems between the various communities, and the different cultures are shared in the town's schools.

Gravesend may seem to have died in some dimensions of its history. But that should not detract from its most remarkable post-war achievement. Citing an Asian joke, Bedi remarks that Sikhs are like potatoes, able to grow anywhere. And yet the elders at the Guru Nanak Day Centre certainly miss some aspects of the Punjabi way of life. Bedi mentions the loss of the traditional courtyard with its 'people tree', where 'the community got together in the late afternoon to exchange news and gossip and play cards'. In the early days, when the Gummers were still at St George's, people may indeed have wondered why the Indians speak so loudly. 'It's not because they're angry or having an argument,' says Bedi, but because they are used to 'standing on the rooftop and shouting across the rooftop: "All right, John? Are you all right?"'

After talking with Shaminder Bedi, I headed back to the riverside where I found various old guns, the ruins of Henry VIII's fortifications, and the offices of the Port of London Authority, which still runs its river pilots from the end of the Royal Pier. I walked past the old Trinity Mission, which was opened in the 1870s to provide for emigrants aboard the ships that once stood at anchor here awaiting the winds that would carry them off to the new world. It is now a private house, restored and owned by an enthusiastic conservationist, who told me that General Gordon himself used to come here to run Bible classes for emigrant children.

Nobody was showing much concern for the souls of the young white boys I encountered a little further on, hanging about a bench just past the little bay where Gravesend's long since vanished shrimp boats used to land their catches. Numerous feminist pundits have written, sometimes a little too gleefully, of the crisis of the young white working class male; and here were some prize specimens of the type, full of empty menace as they tried to put a shine on their own redundancy. These young lads looked as if they would make short work of a 'people tree'. As for the river which once sustained their town, they told me it meant nothing to them at all.

It was a saddening observation, especially since, in this old place of landfall and departure, the water of the Thames has long been a mirror in which every age finds its own prospects reflected. In Joseph Conrad's time, water was a rewarding friend to man and enterprise, the element 'to which men have always been prone to trust themselves'. Full of possibility, the imperial sea also filled towns like Gravesend with epic stories of the kind that were remembered by Charles Dickens, who lived nearby at Gad's Hill and only had to gaze into his glowing fireplace on New Year's Eve to feel such ghostly 'incidents of travel rise round me from all the latitudes and longitudes of the globe'.[15] These jumbled sagas of ice and tropical fire told of piracy, convicts and cannibalism. They mixed Columbus's first glimpse of the new world with lurid testimony from the dark continent of Africa: starvation, white slavery, explorers caged among gory horrors in Abyssinia, well-born English women shipwrecked on remote shores and then glimpsed with their infants years later, weeping outside 'a savage hut far in the interior'.

Nowadays the biggest story on the Thames makes a post-industrial virtue out of emptiness. It emphasizes the fact that the river is nothing like as dirty as it once was. The industrial pollutants have been reduced, and some of the estuary's most famous eyesores have disappeared, too. Looking out from Gravesend, you will search in vain for any indication of the dusty cement factories that Conrad saw around Grays, and there's no trace either of the Tilbury Hotel, which once stood by Tilbury passenger terminal on the opposite shore.

This red-brick structure impressed Conrad as a work of 'monstrous ugliness' ('like a mansion of flats [all to let], exiled into these fields out of a street in West Kensington'). It also dismayed George Orwell as he sailed back from Dunkirk in the early 1930s, having endured his stint as a down-and-out '*plongeur*' washing up in Paris hotels. As his boat approached the pier at Tilbury, Orwell was boasting about the virtues of English architecture for the benefit of a young Rumanian couple coming to England for their honeymoon. All was going fine, until that hideous hotel loomed into view with its 'stucco and pinnacles', peering from the shore like an idiot 'staring over an asylum wall'.[16]

Some relics remain in the museum at Grays but few regret the Tilbury Hotel, which was destroyed by a German bomber in the Second World War. Yet there was not much else for those cavorting Gravesend lads to see as they gazed out from their bench by the water. No forest of masts, to be sure. No cruising yawls like Conrad's 'Nellie', no shrimp boats boiling their catch in 'Bawley' Bay by the Trinity Mission, and no clusters of brown-sailed Thames barges either. Had they felt so inclined, they might have counted the vast container vessels coming in and out of Tilbury Docks. At that time, there were also 'Bovril boats' sailing out on every tide to remind onlookers that, while the Thames may long have been the artery of London, it has always also been its sphincter. Already scheduled for closure under EC regulations, these vessels were in the last year of a service that, for more than a century, had been carrying concentrated sewage sludge from the works at Cross Ness, and dispersing it at sea. Like so many engines of environmental transgression in our age, they were painted a nice shade of ecological green.

EAST TILBURY: A New Start with the Batamen

A slight mist hangs over the salty marsh grass, and the stillness is intensified rather than broken by the sounds that interrupt it: the deep pulsing of passing container ships, the shrilling of waders at the water's edge, and a single bell, tolling dolorously from a buoy in Gravesend Reach.

Washed-up traffic cones poke up in their characteristic way through the tidal mud, and a building of sorts still stands at Coalhouse Point, too. A gaunt, two-tier structure of brick and concrete clinging to a rusted metal frame, East Tilbury's radar station is defunct, and most of its graffiti is unexceptional too. Yet, among the chalked and fading declarations of undying love, I noticed a more abstract statement of loyalty: 'British by birth. English by the grace of God'. I couldn't decide whether those words were written by a passing racist or a perfectly decent fellow whose aberrations extended to no more than a liking for football, milky tea and vacuum-packed ham.

'And this also has been one of the dark places on earth.' Those deeper lines were spoken by Marlowe, the sea-going narrator of Joseph Conrad's *Heart of Darkness*. He was imagining the Thames estuary as it appeared to the Roman, advancing in his trireme to land in a swamp, march through unyielding woods, and feel the 'utter savagery' of the wilderness around him. You can still sense that remoteness on the shore at Coalhouse Point, even though there is nothing left of the four Romano-British huts of wattle and daub that archaeologists once found in this vicinity. It has been suggested that the Romans had a ferry in this place, and even that Emperor Claudius crossed the Thames here shortly after the Roman invasion of AD43. But there is no evidence to support the latter speculation, and it seems most unlikely considering the width of the river, and the fact that Claudius came with elephants as well as the Praetorian Guard.

Yet it has not only been for the Romans that the Thames was a distant northern outpost at the far-flung edge of a disintegrating empire. Even in modern times, East Tilbury was to be colonized by a tribe of people who called themselves Batamen, and who built their main encampment a couple of miles inland.

To reach it, we must head north past the squat fortifications of Coalhouse Fort, constructed in 1861 on the orders of General Gordon who was then responsible for the estuary's defences, and also the battered church of St Katherine. The latter is a weird-looking building, thanks partly to the cannons of the Dutch warships which knocked down its tower in 1667, and partly to the voluntary endeavours of the soldiers who were stationed here during the First World War. Having set about rebuilding the tower, they were apparently ordered to desist when some officious VIP. came by and started enquiring after official permissions.[1] Their dedication stone is in place, but the tower that was meant to rise above it never got much higher than the first window. Capped off at about the height of a modern bungalow, it can be counted the first of East Tilbury's many flat roofs.

The Bata shoe factory stands at the centre of a modernist company town, created by Czech colonists in East Tilbury in the 1930s.

Previous pages
An old lightship rots on the site of the former pleasure beach at Grays, Essex. The Elizabeth II Suspension Bridge at Dartford is visible far right. The overturned ship is the *Arco Arun*, a bulk carrier that sank here in 1998.

Visible over hedge and fields, the Batamen's main centre of activities is a factory complex. The many large and assertively modern blocks are painted white and blue, and the word BATA is emblazoned in red letters on the water tank above the most prominent. The clock above the gatehouse marks the importance of time to this industrial enterprise, and there are many fine trees in the grounds, including poplars, which the early Batamen are said to have planted in order to disperse the water that still gathered in their stretch of former marshland.

If cheap mass-produced shoes are your thing, then East Tilbury is a place of greatness. Wellington boots, school shoes and army boots once poured through the gates by the ton, but you would search in vain for a successor to the sensible ladies' shoe called 'Top Form' or for the popular Bata football boot that was once sold as 'Cup Tie Continental'.

Nowadays, the buildings are run down and mostly empty. Yet Bata's production continues, albeit on a much reduced scale. It begins in a small design studio where a couple of men with the demeanour of pre-industrial craftsmen carve the originals for a gloriously freakish gumboot – perfect for any child who ever suffered the urge to wear a frog's face or a dinosaur on each foot. Nearby, a small conveyorized production line is in the process of 'slush-moulding' a batch of pink children's boots for a well-known retail chain. Other Batafolk sit further down the line: putting in the lining, or perhaps cutting a patch out of the new boots so that the all-important bought-in replica of Mickey Mouse's face can be mounted in the toes. Here was the industrialized system of mass production often known as 'Fordism', but it seemed to have dwindled back, almost to the level of a primitive folk art.

In his office, the Managing Director of British Bata, Peter Nicholls, admits that the East Tilbury operation is now only 'a pimple on the bum' of the global Bata operation. He employs 150 workers, not the three or four thousand of old. Indeed, he was in the process of negotiating the sale of the factory and all its associated land to a developer. New gates were being installed to mark off the modest cluster of buildings that British Bata will continue to rent from the

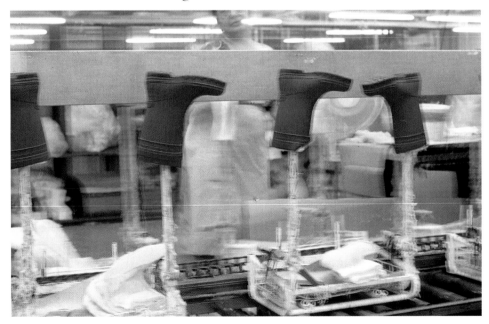

Having pioneered the industrial production of shoes, Bata's conveyorised factory now 'slush-moulds' rubber boots.

new owner, but despite the best efforts of everyone involved, no one can prevent the long-term future of British Bata from curling into the shape of a question mark.

You would have to be blind to drive through East Tilbury village without recognizing that something quite extraordinary has happened here. The recent houses could be anywhere, but Peter Nicholls, who offered to show me around, headed straight for the streets making up what is still known as the 'Czech Village'. Built to accommodate the 'Batamen', these are laid out on a grid system, and the houses are unmistakably middle-European and Modernist. Each of these identical flat-roofed industrial boxes sits in its own little garden, but the slightly bigger ones, intended for managers, have balconies and built-in garages, too.

At the centre of this unconventional settlement stands a vast rectangular block called Stanford House. Now given over to flats and shops, this was once BATA Community House: a considerable works hotel, which also included accommodation for single people, several restaurants and a spacious ballroom, where Bata people used to dance in the formal manner of their times.

Sadly, new worlds are overwhelmed and die just as easily as old ones. A caved-in carpet shop just around the corner turns out once to have been a

purveyor of milkshakes and 'expresso' – a 'coffee bar' which was prominently featured in the leaflets with which the company once sought to attract young workers. There's a war memorial, sports grounds, a medical centre, and a school, now run by the council. But Nicholls also points out many amenities that no longer exist. As the man in charge over recent years, he's had to put an end to flower beds and children's play areas. He's had to fill in the swimming pool, close down Bata College, where the art of conveyorized shoe production was once taught, and demolish empty properties in order to clear sites for sale. He's had to implement huge rent increases and then dispose of those modernist company houses – selling them to tenants at preferential rates, or unloading them on private companies or housing associations. It's a hard business, this thing called 'managing change', but it had to be done – notwithstanding the fact that Thurrock council came along and, to Bata's amazement, declared the Czech village a conservation area and made the oldest of Bata's redundant factory blocks a listed building.

One thing that has not been disposed of is the statue mounted on a grey stone plinth among formal hedges near the factory's main gate. The bronze hero who gazes out from this vantage point is Tomas Bata.

In the words of a company historian, it was Tomas Bata who did for the shoe what Henry Ford had already done for the motor car.[2] Said to have been descended from nine generations of artisan shoemakers, Bata was born in the Moravian town of Zlín in 1867. Dreaming of gentlemanly prosperity, he started with two sewing machines in a small rented house on the town square. An idealist who once claimed to have become a socialist after reading Tolstoy and Zola, he saw industrialization as a means of achieving social reform as well as enormous personal wealth.

Tomas Bata built up a massive factory at Zlín, becoming one of the greatest industrial capitalists in his country. He imported American working methods, agitated his own workers into forming a union, and drew up a 'Moral Testament' which placed the enterprise at the centre of the commonwealth and declared it responsible for uplifting the countryside around it. Business was projected as a service for the democratic age. Governed by the edict that 'the customer is king', Bata's enterprise would give dignity to ordinary men and women, offering them cheap but stylish shoes that would wear well and increase the wearer's status and self-confidence.

'The Bata System' is said to have resembled 'the organization of a modern democratic state'. Believing that industry should be the spreader of 'the Good Life', Tomas introduced profit-sharing systems and proudly claimed to pay his workers better than any other company in the country. Convinced that 'modern industry cannot be built by proletarians', he developed his own college for young employees. The Bataman was never a boy, so Tomas Bata insisted, but a man who earned his keep from the very start.

Not content with creating a factory that he hoped would produce 100,000 pairs of shoes a day, Tomas Bata stood for election as Mayor of Zlín and then set about rebuilding his town from scratch. It was a bright vision of a new industrial order, pursued with impatient disregard for tradition and also for the Communist critics whom Tomas Bata reckoned were more interested in magnifying misery than in bringing about authentic renewal. It was one of his credos that 'You cannot raise strong children in an apartment house'. Moreover, as the town architect F.K.L. Gahura is said to have told his colleague, Vladimir Karfík, 'The Chief believes the man who has a flat in a building with a garden is more stable, and instead of following politics would rather potter about in the garden or sit out on the lawn, so he doesn't go to the pub or political meetings'.[3]

Zlín became a modernist garden city, unique to this day as the only Constructivist city in the world. The plan was full of straight lines, reflecting Bata's belief that 'Whoever shortens roads stretches life'. Determined that buildings should be cheap, quick to build and disposable after their time was done, he used the same industrial principles he had applied to shoes – developing a 'total concept' and a set of architectural blueprints which could be employed over and over again. The British Bata factory at East Tilbury was reputedly full of philosophers in its heyday. But none can have rivalled Tomas, who had his sayings inscribed in huge letters on the wall surrounding the factory in Zlín: 'A wise man does at the beginning what a fool must do at the end.' Or again: 'Buildings are but heaps of bricks and mortar, machines are but piles of steel; only men can give them life.' That one was written at the top of the central electrical plant which powered some 20,000 machines throughout the factory.

At the Bata Celebration of 1 May 1931, Tomas urged the assembled Batamen to think globally: 'Let us not be afraid of the future. Half of the people in the world are walking barefoot and barely five per cent of mankind is well shod.' He reiterated the point the following year: 'Millions of people are still barefoot in this world! It is to be regretted that we do not yet know how to create trade relations with them!'

Built to architectural blueprints brought over from the Czech Republic, Bata's disposable factory and village are now highly regarded by conservationists.

It was with that mission in mind that the Batamen started to travel from Zlín. Tomas, who was an early exponent of flying, cruised around over Italy and North Africa, Palestine and India, eyeing up the bare-footed masses and selecting likely places for new factories. He and his pioneering Batamen favoured open sites, where they could set up their own total system from scratch: factory, industrial village, distribution and retailing operation and all. The buildings and industrial methods may have been identical from one country to the next, but Tomas favoured autonomy for the plants in different countries and regions. His empire was generated according to the unconventional principle he called 'world-wide decentralized business'.

'Today this nation buried its hero.' That was the sentiment with which the Czech Republic buried this airborne Icarus of the modern shoe, after he fell from the sky in a fatal aircrash in 1932. However, the migration of the Batamen was not arrested by this unexpected disaster. Thomas, the son of Tomas, took over, and in 1933 the company bought an old steamship, which had been rusting for several years in Marseilles, filled it with shoes, manufacturing machinery, equipment for retail stores, pigs, chickens and a vast boiler for vulcanizing shoes. They then boarded forty-three graduates from the Bata School for Young Men at Zlín, and sailed for India and Java. Other Batamen were transported to the West Indies, where they were soon fighting off an invasion of cheap Japanese plimsolls. Wherever the young Batamen went, they took capital from the home company in Zlín, along with machines, building plans and technical skills. It is said that they sang old Moravian folk songs as they and their local labourers worked. They founded 'Batanagar' in India, 'Batawa' in Canada, 'Batapur' in Pakistan, 'Kalibata' in Indonesia – building up 'a sort of civilization somehow different from the commercial and industrial civilization of the time'.

It was partly with an eye on Britain's imperial markets that Bata first came to East Tilbury in 1932, acquiring a considerable stretch of marshland with a few houses that were soon disposed of and, as one elder remembers, 'nothing but a few pea-fields' for anybody to work in. Tomas Bata is said to have approved the site and come to terms with the farmer who owned it, but East Tilbury's factory and 'Czech village' were built after the founder's death. The Batamen arrived, recruited some young natives from Grays and other nearby towns, and set to work communicating by sign language as they constructed a new world. Here, as at Zlín, the garden village was built under the slogan 'living separately – working together'. Everything was designed, right down to the cherry trees planted in every Bataman's front garden; and life in this dramatically renovated pocket of Essex was soon being conducted in the proven Bata way.

There were town meetings, sports facilities, and company shops that sold produce from the Bata farm. There was a Bata fire brigade and even a Bata milkround. The *Bata Record* reported on Bata sports events, celebrated the marriages of Batamen and Batagirls, and printed such things as the BATA ABC – 'A is for ambition by which we are fired. B is for Bata by which it is inspired'. It is said that just about everyone in Thurrock has worked at Bata at one time or another: some hated the mixture of industrial routine and social paternalism and left as soon as they could, but others stayed for a lifetime, settling for a secure job, a place in the envied Bata village, and a wage that didn't seem at all bad by local standards.

British Bata's business thrived through the Second World War, thanks partly to conveyorized production of the British army boot. East Tilbury formed its own 'Bata Army', a detachment of the Home Guard in which the managing director of that time, John Tusa, father of the well-known broadcaster, served as a private. There were galas and concerts for members of the Czech forces in Britain, and the ballroom at Bata House resounded with the 'songs of the homeland'.

That same pattern of national loyalty would be resumed in 1968, when Czechs fleeing the Russian tanks were welcomed at East Tilbury and given work and assistance. By then, British Bata had a workforce of some 3500 recruited from all over the world – elsewhere in Britain, Ireland, Europe, India, Pakistan and South Africa. Vic Attard puts his arrival down to a company recruiter who came to Malta looking for workers in 1966 – a few friends signed up, and Mr Attard decided to follow as soon as word got back about the Beatles, miniskirts and other attractions of 'swinging' London: 'Here I come I said… You can't stop me.' And he's been in East Tilbury ever since.

Just across the road from the old Community House, the Bata Cinema used to run three different programmes every week. In May 1962, it was screening *The World of Suzie Wong*, with an 'emotional' American drama called *Back Street* due to top the bill on Sunday and a 'much more interesting' picture called *I Passed for White* coming on Wednesday.

But Bata's age has passed; and the cinema, which has been restored with a grant from English Heritage, is now East Tilbury Village Hall, where the Bata elders meet for tea, Bingo and sometimes line-dancing, too. The day I called in, they didn't need much prompting to start looking back fondly on life as it was before. They remembered the Christmas voucher, adding that, of course, it did have to be spent in the company's own outlets in Community House. There would be £5 in a money box for every new born Batachild, and no-one had objected to the fact that a penny for Dr Barnado's Homes was deducted at source from the wage. The safety of the old Czech village was so taken for granted that people going away on their annual holidays would leave their back doors unlocked.

The Bata system involved a profit-sharing scheme which, according to a company handbook from the fifties, was 'based on the assumption that in the course of time the enterprise will be owned and largely controlled by the people who work in it'. But somehow, that never happened. Nobody likes to moan, but one man, who had put in forty years of service, counted up his entire annual pension and arrived at a paltry sum that could hardly buy a meal for two in a smart London restaurant.

These Batafolk are making a go of living in the ruins of a community that once promised to see them through to the end. 'I saw the world,' says Mr Purkiss from his chair, just behind the old Bata Hotel. He became a Bataman in 1936, and was among those who went to Zlín to be trained in industrial methods and also the Czech language. On his return, he helped to introduce conveyorized production at Tilbury, and then went on to do the same in Australia and elsewhere. Reg Fields now sticks to his patch, too – life is so localized that he has to struggle to remember his area code. Yet he also was sent out to Zlín in 1933 – 'a fantastic place', as he says, still shaking his head in amazement at the fact that he, a working-class lad from Thurrock, should ever have learned how to ski.

So what happened to pull all this apart? I put this question to Peter Nicholls, the Managing Director, who lives in the real world in which idealistic businesses fall as well as rise. To begin with, he suggests, the amount of national autonomy fostered in Bata's world system probably stood in the way of developing truly global brands of the kind that have become so important for other manufacturers. Bata was once proud to describe itself as the 'largest exporter of footwear in Great Britain', but the colonial markets, which were once so profitable, dried up thanks partly to the policy of global decentralization under which new Bata plants were opened in Africa and the Caribbean. Perhaps the Bata name also fell too far down market as it reached out towards the masses. As for the Bata shops that once traded across Britain as family stores, they were sold off to Sears, and not very advantageously.

Asked what the future holds for East Tilbury, now that it is no longer sustained by Bata, Mr Nicholls hopes that it doesn't revert to type as 'the dumping ground of England' – a no-go zone in which 'they sometimes dig a hole and call it Lakeside'. This may sound excessively gloomy, but Thurrock has long been so seriously devoted to waste disposal that it is hard to go for a walk without falling into a rubbish tip or landfill site. As for its main town, having been so thoroughly demolished by its council in the sixties and seventies, Grays is freely described as 'a dump' even by its own disappointed inhabitants. One of the few guidebooks written about this southern stretch of Essex even suggests that Thurrock may not have been named after 'Thor's Oak' after all. The alternative root is 'thorrocke' – said to mean the place in the bottom of a ship 'wherein ys gathered all the fylthe'.[4]

As for the old radar station down at Coalhouse Point, Nicholls imagines that a new road bridge might one day land in that place where the Romans are said to have made their crossing. I must have raised an eyebrow at this, because he insisted that East Tilbury would be an excellent site for crossing the Thames – perfect for those who wanted to skirt London and get through Thurrock in a hurry with the help of a new outer peripheral route connected to the M25.

FOBBING: Peasants in Revolt

The village of Fobbing stands on a wooded rise above the Essex marshes. Nowadays, this is to say that it looks out over two vast and flaring oil refineries: Shell Haven, which is soon to be closed, and BP's Coryton, which stands on a 1500-acre site previously used by Kynoch and Company, another explosives factory which closed down after the First World War. Upriver, the representative Thames pub might be 'The Wild Duck' or 'The Compleat Angler', but in these parts it is called 'The Catcracker', and its sign shows an oil refinery blazing in a ruddy sunset with the apparatus that every local recognizes as a 'Catalytic Cracker' very much to the fore.

There was once marsh fever here, too. It accounted for a 'strange decay' of the female sex observed and perhaps also exaggerated by Daniel Defoe, who passed through 'this damp part of the world' in the early 1720s. In his book *A Tour through the Whole Island of Great Britain*, Defoe recorded that 'it was very frequent to meet with men that had had from five or six, to fourteen or fifteen wives'. Indeed, he was informed that one marshland farmer in the area was living with his twenty-fifth wife, while his son, who was still only thirty-five, was already getting through his fourteenth. Asked to explain this dire phenomenon, one participating farmer told Defoe:

> That they being bred in the marshes themselves, and season'd to the place, did pretty well with it; but that they always went up into the hilly country, or to speak their own language into the uplands for a wife: That when they took the young lasses out of the wholesome and fresh air, they were healthy, fresh and clear, and well; but when they came out of their native air into the marshes among the fogs and damps, there they presently chang'd their complexion, got an ague or two, and seldom held it above half a year, or a year at most; and then, said he, we go to the uplands again; and fetch another; so that marrying of wives was reckon'd a kind of good farm to them.

The Essex marshes. Agricultural workers sowing rice grass in a waterlogged field near Manningtree in 1932.

One mid-century surveyor of Essex's 'Forgotten Thameside' declared Fobbing to be 'wrapped in an atmosphere as mysterious as any of the strange towns pictured by Algernon Blackwood'. Served by a winding tidal creek, its harbour was surely the smallest in Essex, and one that had been much favoured by smugglers. Turn your back on the flaring oil refineries and it is still possible to appreciate Fobbing's elevation over the fatal marsh. The 'rook-infested elms' may have gone, but the grey stone tower of Fobbing church still pierces the sky above a village that seems to clamber up towards it from the defunct brick fields on either side of its lost harbour. As for the rising 'cliff' on which the village stands, this has the added advantage of being a real hill, not a man-made construction of landscaped rubbish like many of the apparently natural slopes that rise around the estuary.

Nobody has exactly moved Fobbing rectory, yet the capacious house next to St Michael's can no longer be said to sit 'in the world of Trollope, with its garden parties and croquet'. The present vicar, Mrs Lawner Smith, lives with her accountant husband a few miles away in Stanford-le-Hope; and the building that was home to her celebrated seventeenth-century predecessor, the mathematician John Pall, is now an 'old rectory' belonging to the family of George Walker, the boxing promoter and once bankrupted businessman who has been busy relaunching his operations in Russia since the collapse of his Brent Walker leisure empire.

In the early sixties, Fobbing was also home to George's brother, the boxer Billy Walker, popularly known as the 'Blond Bomber'. Besides running on the marshes, Billy trained in a converted garage at the rectory ('lovely and quiet'). It might have seemed appropriate, in that sleepy place, to carry on with the English way of fighting, a gentlemanly approach organized around the Queensberry Rules, which favoured the straight left hand and right cross. But, as Billy Walker remembers, too many English boxers got walloped by the Yanks during the war. So he tried to adopt the American style, which prioritized hooking and throwing lots of punches. A famously persistent and aggressive fighter who sparred with Joe Bugner and fought Henry Cooper and other giants of that time, Billy Walker made good even without winning any major championships, punching his way out of poverty in the classic downriver style. He was recently back from abroad when I met him, and planning a move to Guildford.

The thought of boxing in the rectory may not have pleased every inhabitant of Fobbing, and yet the Walkers could certainly have claimed a local precedent for their pugilistic activities. Long before the oil refineries were built in the 1950s, the marshes below Fobbing were favoured by boxers as well as wild-fowlers. Many illegal prize fights are said to have been fought here: if the law found the spot, the fighters and their audience simply took to the river and sailed off to another remote place where they would complete the contest ('handy if you're losing', observes Billy Walker). The most celebrated of these fights was the 1862 Heavy Weight Championship of Great Britain, in which Tom Sayers slugged it out with Jem Mace in what is said to have been the last prize fight to have been held in the open air.

And if that didn't provide the Walkers with precedent enough, they could also have cited the fact that, in the fourteenth century, Fobbing was a cradle – perhaps even a 'storm centre' – of the Peasants' Revolt.

Introduced under Richard II in 1377, the first poll tax in English history was intended to extract wealth from 'every lay person of either sex older than fourteen – except for notorious paupers'. A second tax was introduced in 1379, and another in 1380. The returns were very poor, however, and in March 1381 poll tax commissioners were appointed to secure the missing payments. So it was that Sir Thomas Bampton came to Essex, established a base at Brentford and demanded that the people of neighbouring townships pay up.

The river seems to have been a conveyance of discontent, for, as the Victoria county history says of the revolt, 'the portion of the county most implicated was along the Thames shore'. Resistance is said to have been stirred up by Thames fishermen, probably abetted by fishmongers in the City of London. But the people of Fobbing appear to have been responsible for the first actual riots. Refusing to pay their supposed dues to Commissioner Bampton, they took to the woods when threatened by him. In one version, it was the Fobbing baker, a man named Thomas Baker, who began to 'exhort and ally himself with the men of his village'. Whether or not Baker was 'the first mover and later the chief leader', the Fobbing villagers made common cause with others from nearby villages of Corringham and Stanford-le-Hope, and then, in a body of about a hundred, confronted Bampton with their refusal to pay.

Bampton tried to arrest them, but the protesters rose against his officers, and threatened to kill Bampton and his two sergeants-at-arms. Bampton fled, and the rebels extended their agitation to other towns and villages. Soon a horde of some 5000 peasants, reputedly 'of the lowest sort', was marching through manors and villages towards London. Armed with sticks, rusty swords and, according to one mocking observer, a single arrow which only had one feather, they burned out those who wouldn't support them, beheaded three of Bampton's clerks, and then pressed on brandishing their victims' heads on poles and promising the same treatment to all lawyers, believing that there would be 'no liberty until they were gone'.

Richard II sailing down the Thames to meet the rebels; manuscript illustration of the Peasants' Revolt from the *Chroniques de Froissart*.

By 3 June, the Essex rebels had made common cause with others in Kent. Some marched on Dartford, storming Rochester Castle and then Maidstone, where Wat Tyler was appointed leader with a man called Jack Straw, who some have tried to claim for Fobbing, as his deputy. Having marched on Canterbury, where they burned out the Archbishop, Simon Sudbury, the rebels converged on London – some 50,000 advancing along the south bank of the river, and 60,000 along the Essex side. The fourteen-year-old king, Richard II, came down the river on his barge, but retreated rather than disembarking into the crowds at Rotherhithe. So the rebels assaulted London, firing John of Gaunt's Savoy Palace in Fleet Street, breaking open the prisons of Marshalsea, Fleet and Newgate, beheading lawyers and foreign merchants, and besieging the tower, where the king 'anxiously and sadly' remained.

Richard eventually met the rebels in fields east of London at Mile End, agreeing to make the reforms they demanded ('that henceforward no man should be a serf nor make homage or any type of service to any lord…') But this capitulation did not prevent an Essex contingent of rebels from breaking into the tower and beheading both Archbishop Sudbury, who was also the Chancellor of the Exchequer, and the Treasurer, Sir Robert Hales. At a further meeting with the King at Smithfield, Wat Tyler demanded that, in addition to previous concessions, church lands should be divided up among commoners. But there was then a fracas, and Tyler was fatally stabbed by William Walworth – whose knife is commemorated in the crest of the City of London to this day.

After this, the rebels capitulated, and dispersed peacefully when Richard agreed to honour his promises if they did so. Shortly afterwards he raised an army and marched on the disintegrated rebellion. Petitioned by Essex men at Waltham Abbey, he dispatched them saying, 'Villans you were and villans you are; in bondage you shall abide, and that not your old bondage, but one incomparably worse.' Fobbing's Thomas Baker was among those who were hanged. The others were lucky to get back to their villages empty-handed.

Six hundred years later, I am walking around a large and crudely decorated metal arch in the village playground with two local residents, Terry and Tina Scott. A work of public art, I observe. 'So we are told,' fires Tina, remembering the day when 'a lorry pulled up with this monstrosity on its back'. 'I couldn't quite believe my eyes – speechless really. It was like something from out of space, like something a child would make at play school… We were expecting a tasteful monument of some description, a bench or a birdbath, or some such thing, and then this landed… The man who put this thing together, obviously had a very vivid imagination.'

This is a familiar story around the estuary by now. State intervention may have come on a grand scale in the fifties and sixties, but by the time Fobbing's unwanted monument to the Peasants' Revolt came along, the public authorities that once tried to demolish their way into the future had entered a Lilliputian phase. With the old levers of power sold off or derelict, councils were left trying to lift their neighbourhoods with no heavier equipment than new litter bins, bollards and fake Victorian lamp-posts. It was in this climate that public art underwent a renaissance: its symbolic 'interventions' being as attractive to commercial sponsors as they were to councillors who had not got over their appetite for visible public works.

When the people of a locality are successfully involved, public art may be appreciated as better than camouflage on a blighted reality. But it takes more than 'community consultation' to secure a work of public art on the Thames estuary. Gravesend's mural of rioting watermen makes a shrewd pre-emptive strike against

vandalism, by including large amounts of it in the picture. But Tina and Terry Scott were not for a moment taken in by the various acts of insubordination represented on Fobbing's monument.

Looking at the various names and slogans written into its panels, I find Jack Straw, a leader of the rebellion, only to be told that he is 'Big in history, but not in the present'. The slogan 'The strong shall help the weak' may express an admirable sentiment but, says Tina Scott, it has 'nothing to do with us at all'. As for the increased 'bondage' that Richard II promised the peasants, I'm afraid that only occasioned the unexpected revelation that the *News of the World* had printed a saucy article, exposing a claimed wife-swapping circle in Fobbing.

Ben Coode-Adams' controversial monument to the Peasants' Revolt, in Fobbing playground.

Fobbing is a predominantly Tory village in the Labour district of Thurrock, and there can be little doubt that its monument to the Peasants' Revolt was itself commissioned as an instrument of Essex class war. In 1981, the people of Fobbing had tried to persuade Thurrock Council to commemorate the 600th anniversary of the insurrection by mounting a memorial in the village. At that time, however, the council had refused, apparently believing that as a Tory outpost in a Labour borough, Fobbing was wealthy enough to pay for its own monument. So a plaque was mounted in the pub, commending those fourteenth-century rebels as if they had been early free-marketeers holding out against the collectivist state.

All this changed, however, once Margaret Thatcher introduced the poll tax. By 1990, it was the Labour Council that was suddenly very keen to erect a monument on Fobbing's village green. And they wanted one very quickly, so that its unveiling could coincide with an anti-poll tax march planned to depart from the village. So some preliminary designs were commissioned, and the artist, Ben Coode-Adams, was hurriedly set to work.

The completed work was brought in by road, but as far as the people of Fobbing were concerned, it might as well have been beamed down from outer space. As Tina Scott recalls, 'It looked like something out of *Star Wars*…it just landed on the green.' The unveiling of this shiny metal artwork impressed Fobbing as little better than a provocation. Coachloads of anti-poll tax demonstrators were in attendance, and the council had even tied red balloons to the top of the thing. The people of Fobbing were loud in their objection. Terry and Tina remember the artist looking terrified, and staying close to the police throughout. The Mayor of Thurrock, a Labour stalwart called Councillor Bidmead, insisted that the sculpture would only be moved 'over my dead body', and then went on to denounce the Fobbing rebels as 'Philistines'.

By the next day, a 'For Sale' sign had appeared on the work, and the bolts securing it to its concrete plinth were miraculously loosened. Nobody in Fobbing resorted to open vandalism but, in Tina's phrase, 'it did fall apart quite well'. It was rumoured that the locals might encourage gypsies to steal the unwanted artwork and flog it off as scrap metal, so the council returned to weld the thing firmly in place. A group called the 'Friends of Fobbing' organized a petition, signed by the majority of the village, demanding that the monument be moved.

So, in the end, it was shifted to its isolated spot at the side of the playground. On 1 June 1990, Tina Scott was featured denouncing this 'piece of junk' as the *Daily Telegraph* reported on the victory of Fobbing's 'twentieth-century "peasants' revolt"'. Neither she nor Terry have softened in their criticism since. What they really should have done, says Terry, is to take the money given to the artist and knock it off the poll tax, or the Community Charge as supporters much preferred it to be called.

CANVEY ISLAND: Paradise in Mud

I am standing high over the water on a gangway leading to an oddly perched blue shack belonging to the harbour master, and I'm talking with a man who can't stand still. There's a speedy stare in his eyes and he marches back and forth as he speaks. Even when the rest of him seems securely propped against the handrail, his head keeps cannoning about like a snooker ball.

'Haven't been here for years,' says Wilko Johnson, staring across the water and mud of Holehaven Creek to the vast oil refinery beyond, and remembering the Canvey Island he knew as a boy. After recalling that he used to catch crabs from the end of the jetty down there, he turns back towards Canvey and points north towards the marshes behind the sea-wall. It's more built up now, he explains, but in the sixties that was one of those wild and informal areas where adolescents could go to discover themselves. Asking for a pencil, Canvey's guitar hero scribbles out some lyrics to show how, in one of the last songs he wrote before falling out with his island friends in the band Dr Feelgood, he turned this battered industrial wilderness into 'Paradise'.

> *Went out walking, I recall*
> *Me and my best girl, along the wall*
> *In the long grass, side by side*
> *Where the big ships, go gliding by, go gliding by*
> *Skylark singing, in the sun*
> *Something told me, she's the one*
> *When I looked down, into her eyes*
> *I saw pictures, of Paradise, of Paradise, of Paradise.*

Wilko Johnson is certainly not the only rock musician who has found himself feeling unaccountably shaky at the height of his cult, but his song 'Paradise' is a Canvey Island classic. Dating from 1977, it finds Wilko at his 'darkest hour', fighting his way through pharmaceutical and sexual excess, to recall the innocent 'prelapsarian' simplicities of the life he once knew in this muddy stretch of Essex. The memory of Canvey's oil refinery looms up over this 'dark night of the soul' like so many forbidding 'towers of Babylon', and there's a chorus in which 'TV screen' is rhymed not just with 'look so mean' and being 'seventeen', but with 'Irene, Irene'. She's the abandoned woman who found her strangely boosted man 'lost inside a dream' and then 'brought me back Irene, Irene'. All these years later, Irene is still standing at Wilko Johnson's side, or rather sitting with him at a table in the Lobster Smack, where he explains that she makes all his decisions, and then passes her the menu so that she can choose him a steak sandwich to chase down the whisky with which he is preparing himself for this thing called lunch.

Talking with Wilko Johnson (left) by the Harbour Master's office overlooking Holehaven Creek, Canvey Island.

My first information about Canvey Island's guitar hero emerged from Newcastle upon Tyne, where Wilko Johnson went to study English in the late sixties. Known as John Wilkinson in those days, he is remembered as an ardent, not to say loud-mouthed, leftist. At that time, student fashion had much to do with whether the shoulders of your dark-blue donkey-jacket were plain, or covered with seriously worker-like shiny leatherette panels. Wilko had the patches, and, even in the hard land of the Geordie, his proletarian standing was con-siderably enhanced by his pronounced Canvey accent. After Newcastle University, he found his way home to Canvey, via India, and engaged in a bit of supply-teaching. Some time in 1972, he got out the old Fender Stratocaster that he had bought in his teens, with Irene's help, and joined some old Canvey Island friends in forming Dr Feelgood. They played hard and simple R&B as Wilko recalls: 'a very basic kind of music' from 'a very basic kind of place'. 'We come from Canvey Island, know what I mean.' Within a few years Dr Feelgood were being fêted all over the place as 'The greatest local band in the world'.

But is Canvey Island a lost Paradise for anyone except Wilko Johnson? Certainly not according to any genteel account of what makes a significant landscape or town. From that perspective, Canvey Island is the kind of place where you really notice the adverts posted by the Samaritans, and perhaps even think of noting down the freephone number in case you get stuck here for a few nights. 'Bad Trip', as one bus shelter announces. 'Come in and Have a Faith Lift', says a sign by the church, renewing the polite visitor's desire to jump off the sea wall.

How, as the accidental visitor is likely to wonder, can anyone ever have mistaken this stretch of mediocre suburban sprawl for a holiday resort? Go to the southernmost point, and you find that holidaymakers are still camping out in what feels like the most dreary kind of housing estate. They may have to scramble up a high wall to get so much as a glimpse of the muddy estuarial sea. The beach may be of dubious semi-industrial status, and the view dominated by the huge petro-chemical complex on the western side of the island. But none of this deters the stalwarts who still come with buckets and spades, sunbathe and swim out towards the vast container ships.

Canvey Island is a great unsorted jungle of a place, with several different histories all piled up together. Most Canveyites may nowadays be quite at home with the weird juxtapositions that result, but there have been some moments of awkwardness in the past. Wilko Johnson remembers a caravan site on the west of the island. It was right up against the oil-storage depot established near Holehaven in 1938, and, as he recalls, they used to sell picture postcards of it, but not before they had airbrushed out the looming oil tanks — like Stalinists removing purged politicians from photographs of the great leader.

Yet Wilko was certainly on to something when he found Paradise in Canvey. Early paintings of Paradise show tiny islands of beauty, grace and harmony, walled enclosures which are often surrounded by cosmic darkness. Canvey lacks obvious grace and pastoral attraction, but the wall is unmistakably real.

In the beginning Canvey was mud — yet another ague-infested marsh, much of it lying below the level of the high spring tides and endlessly encroached upon by the sea. There is nothing to suggest that 4000 delicately flavoured sheep once grazed here, as Camden reported in 1607, tended by shepherd boys who had small stools fastened to their buttocks to assist them in milking ewes and making cheese in sheds. But the memory of this elemental place survives in Canvey's coat of arms, which bears the motto 'From the sea by the grace of God'. The first comprehensive sea-wall was actually made by Dutch engineers employed in the 1620s by Joas Croppenburg, a wealthy London-based Dutch merchant who received a third of the 3600 reclaimed acres as his reward. There was considerable tension between the Dutch, who set out to create dry land for arable farming, and the native livestock farmers, who needed a higher water level, and also the marshmen who lived by wildfowl.

Originally created by Croppenburg's workers, Canvey's close-knit Dutch Colony has left two characteristically round or octagonal early seventeenth-century thatched cottages, both of which are known as Dutch Cottage. Other residues include a hostile ballad in which the Dutch are accused of turning eels into snakes and even endangering 'good English beer',[5] and also the name of Bread and Cheese Hill in South Benfleet, where Dutch-hating locals (tensions were exacerbated by three Anglo-Dutch wars in the seventeenth century) used to stop men they suspected of being Dutch and make them say 'Bread and Cheese' in order to assess whether their pronunciation justified immediate assault.

In 1887, the walled island of Canvey could still be described as 'purely agricultural', with a population of some three hundred which had been more or less static throughout the century. But agriculture was depressed and the twentieth century was built on other prospects. As the farmers went bankrupt, large parts of the island were bought up by Frederick Hester, a Southend land agent who renamed the island 'Canvey on Sea' and divided it up into plots which he sold to East-Enders with the one restriction that there was to be no industrial development.[6] Within a few years, Canvey was known as the cheapest possible place for a seaside holiday. It became a makeshift Arcadia full of shacks and improvised cabins. Some of the new dwellings were made of recycled bus bodies and railway carriages; others looked as if they had been bashed together out of corrugated iron or woven out of willow and raffia.

Plotland Canvey became a paradise of popular pleasure, an enterprise zone of the ramshackle DIY variety that was the despair of planners and also of the Council for the Preservation of Rural England, an upriver organization, by and large, which, in its Thames Valley Survey of 1929, nevertheless decreed that 'The hut or shack built of temporary materials, and often patched together should not be allowed on the Thames anywhere.'[7] The Canvey urban district council was working to tidy up the plotlands from the mid-twenties. Many shacks became bungalows, as East-End families moved in – a pattern that was greatly increased after the Second World War, when the bombing and its chaotic aftermath made permanent relocation in Canvey seem a sensible option for many who had started out with a summer shack. The planners may never really have recognized it, but Canvey was no longer the remote and ague-ridden wilderness that prompted the heroine of a novel published in 1900 to say 'It's like being dead and buried.'[8] In the words of one local guidebook, it had become 'an Isle of Delight in the Mouth of the Silvery Thames'.

The members of Dr Feelgood were children of that happy migration from East London. The son of a gas-fitter, Wilko Johnson remembers a Canvey Island that was lot more open than it is now. 'When I was a boy it was almost rural really, with open fields and farms.' He remembers not just the oil refineries but a landscape of shacks dotted along untarred roads. Canvey was also more palpably an island. 'When you come on to the island now, you may not realize you're crossing water on to an island. But there was one little old bridge, then, which used to open, and you knew that boats had the right of way over cars. If anyone wanted to sail through, the bridge would open and the traffic would just have to stop.' Canvey felt more remote and cut off – a marshy place of autumnal mists that, of an evening, would surge around you 'kind of like dry ice on *Top of the Pops*'. When he went off the island to grammar school, he found that Canvey had a certain reputation, as if 'there was something a little peculiar about people coming from Canvey'.

Dr Feelgood did nothing to dispel this rumour of marsh-dwelling hardness. Their music was defiantly unsophisticated R&B borrowed from the Mississippi. Canvey still had its old wooden shacks with porches, which might just as well have had a guitar-picker perched on them; and 'if you squint your eyes' in Canvey, 'you can imagine the Thames as a delta'. It wasn't 'exactly Tom Sawyer,' admits Wilko, 'but yeah the Delta… It got reflected in the sound of the music, the lyrics, and things like that…'

As for the Fall that stalks Paradise, that may have come down to the familiar trinity of sex and drugs and rock 'n' roll in Wilko's song 'Paradise'. But there was a wider Canvey precedent there, too. During the plotland era, some visitors had yearned for a cleansing spasm that would sweep away all this ugliness. According to Colin Ward and Dennis Hardy, one government inspector called Canvey 'an abomination…a town of shacks and rubbish… It caters for a particular class of people, and short of total destruction and a new start, little if anything can be done'. The destruction came soon enough, a cleansing assault that looked more like a muddy deluge to the unfortunate islanders who found themselves caught up in it. It happened one freezing night at the very end of January 1953. North-west gales combined with a vast tidal surge to raise the sea some 2 metres above its normal high-tide level. There was terrible trouble all over the east coast, but Canvey was the worst affected area, and fifty-eight islanders died that night, as the 'sunken marsh' area on the east of the island suddenly became 'the basin of death'.[9]

The disaster is vividly remembered by John Lawrence, who keeps a boat-yard by the bridge on to Canvey, overlooking the creek where the Vikings were

Holiday-makers playing leapfrog on the beach at Canvey Island, August 1922.

sorted out back in the ninth century. He was aboard a trawler that night, moored at Leigh-on-Sea. When the tide came up over the wharf, he and his fellows rowed up Leigh High Street, aware that it would be 'a memorable thing' to have done. After that, they went to bed, only to be woken by a policeman who announced that Canvey was flooded and lost to communication, since the phone lines were down, and volunteers were needed to go over and help. So they sailed to Canvey with a skiff in tow, and found a great breach in the wall, and a knot of people standing huddled at its edge.

As Lawrence explains, 'the sea-walls had been totally neglected. The cattle, which used to graze all round them, had trodden them down, and they hadn't been repaired for years.' The tide came over the wall and then washed away the back embankments, causing the whole structure to collapse in several places at once. As they sailed in through the breach, Lawrence and his colleagues passed the drowned bodies of an elderly couple, caught up in a bush, and saw people perched in rows on their bungalow roofs, wind-lashed and freezing in their nightwear 'like sparrows on the ridge'.

Having burst in, the sea stayed put for many hours, only really receding after the next tide. The Essex County Council's history of the flood records the ordeal in terrible detail. Many spent the night clinging desperately to doors or fanlights. Some of the luckier ones were able to sit the night out on their kitchen tables, and one solitary elderly lady survived by stacking a pile of books on her washbasin, and perching there, freezing in pitch darkness, crammed up against the ceiling as the water rose up past her knees. A mother described standing up to her neck in water in her living-room, desperately holding up two infants as they died in her arms.

This sudden deluge was one of Wilko Johnson's earliest memories. He was among the 11,000 islanders who were evacuated. The family stayed for a while with relatives in Sheffield, and came back in time to see steps being taken to dry out the houses that had been filled with water and sludge: 'They had RAF lorries blowing hot air into these cardboard houses of ours.' Canvey had been declared a disaster area, and international aid poured in. Every day at primary school, 'you'd get a packet of raisins from California, a tin of sardines from Norway, and some second-hand toy'. The memory of that flood became one of the ways in which Canvey islanders fixed events in time. Elsewhere – 'in England', as Johnson put it – people may have talked of things that happened before or after the Second World War, but in Canvey Island it was 'before and after the flood…it had a biblical feeling, like an inundation'.

John Lawrence remembers the flood as 'a total devastation of the island'. Until then, Canvey was still predom-inantly a plotlanders' island. But the flood virtually put an end to

Canvey Island flooded in January 1953. Fifty-eight people died after a tidal surge broke through the sea-wall.

the DIY bungalow, and prepared the way for the 'land-grabbers' who started to lay claim to abandoned land. It assisted the advancing house-builders in another way, too. Before the deluge, Canvey 'virtually only had two roads. But they put in flood-relief roads, which opened up all the unmade roads, and then the house-builders moved in…'

'It could be something in the air here,' says Wilko when asked about the Peasants' Revolt. That fourteenth-century rebellion had not found its theme-park by the early seventies, but, for Dr Feelgood, the march on London certainly continued – carried on, as Wilko remembered, with the help of a succession of battered Transit vans. It was 'a bit of a crusade' when the Feelgoods started played the pub circuit in London. They wore cheap old suits, found in Canvey market and kept defiantly filthy in the battle against decadence and over-sophistication. The members of Dr Feelgood were pleased to go over like 'Hiroshima in a pint pot', and even insisted on issuing their first LP only in Mono.

An uncompromising guitar slasher, Wilko also marched on London in another Canvey cause, this time against Occidental Oil. As he put it, 'In the seventies, they were planning to build two huge new refineries here; and the western half of the island would have been more or less covered with them. Of course, the local people didn't take to the idea, and we formed a protest movement. We were doing all sorts of guerrilla tactics, going up to London with coachloads of housewives and kids, and invading the oil companies' offices and demanding answers and stuff like that. But,' he says, gazing out at the vast but never used jetty that still litters the island, 'they still built the bloody thing, or half built the thing, and then something happened in the Middle East, or something, and we've never heard from them since. So thanks a lot, guys.

'Yeah, we marched on London. We sailed on London. We did one thing sailing up the river in a load of boats waving flags. And yeah, they were a little bit scared of us. But there's nothing you can do, actually. If an oil company wants to build something next to your house, an oil company is going to build it. You can't do anything about it.' So says Wilko Johnson, pausing before he adds, 'You've got to try though.'

TILBURY DOCKS:
Last Call for the Socialist River

'Well, after what I saw in Tilbury, and elsewhere, it seems to me we've still got a long way to make up in the matter of sectionalism and regionalism...'

Jack Lindsay, *Rising Tide*

Launched by the London County Council in 1889, the Woolwich Free Ferry service is said to have had its finest hour during the Blitz of 7 September 1940. Targeted for its Royal Docks, Silvertown was ablaze and cut off from the north, and the residents were rescued by a paddle-powered ferry-boat called *Squires* that plied the river throughout that frightful night.[10]

The Woolwich Ferry has yet to be replaced by a bridge, although two are now planned for the area, and it also remains a free service despite the many cost-cutting bureaucrats who must have dreamed of remedying this outstanding lapse in business realism. *Squires* has long since gone, but the defiantly contrary traditions of the old docklands live on in the names of its successors, *John Burns* and *Ernest Bevin*. It's one of the last sights of the socialist Thames, to see these two names passing each other in midstream at the very place where unaccustomed motorists expect London's north

Slowing down on the Free Ferry at Woolwich, where the North and South Circular roads meet.

and south circular roads to meet. Ernest Bevin is remembered as a militant Welsh trade unionist, a dockers' leader among other things, who rose to become Foreign Secretary in Clement Attlee's Labour Cabinet. The Liberal John Burns belonged to an earlier age before the Labour Party was even formed. If you trust a dictionary of quotations, his claim to immortality seems to rest entirely on a single remark he made while defending the Thames against a condescending American who had mocked it as a piddling thing compared with the much larger

Mississippi. England's river, Burns replied, was 'liquid history', and far superior to the merely muddy waters of the new world.

That phrase could have been coined by many more conventional admirers of the imperial river, but Burns was a champion of the poor and unemployed whose radical demands ensured that he was frequently likened to Jack Cade and other rebels of the Peasants' Revolt. Born of working-class Scottish parents in South London in 1858, John Burns's local endeavours had earned him considerable reputation as 'the King of Battersea' by 1889, when he joined the new London County Council and also took up the cause of unskilled workers at the docks of London.

As sites of casual labour, London's docks had long been 'the magnet for those desperately seeking work'.[11] According to one observer, dockers were at that time 'the poorest of the poor, the flotsam and jetsam of the waterside. They were unorganized, despised, even by their fellow workers, without hope or craft.'[12] Beatrice Webb noted the 'abject misery' of the men converging on the dock-gates in hope of work, and accepted the judgement of the School Board Visitor who had reported that 'they are like the circle of the suicides in

Strikers assembling in East India Dock Road before marching on the City of London, 1889.

Dante's *Inferno*: they go round and round within a certain area'. The dockers' leader Ben Tillett described the terrible scenes that happened each morning as hundreds of desperate men congregated in the 'cage' at the dock-gate and fought to catch the eye of a foreman, who might perhaps have a day's work for twenty men: 'Coats, flesh and even ears were torn off. The strong literally threw themselves over the heads of their fellows and battled through the kicking, punching, cursing crowds to the rails of the "cage" which held them like rats – mad human rats.'

In August 1889, the dockers went on strike, inspired by the actions of unskilled match-workers and gas-workers of the previous year. This first major organized strike to hit the London docks started as a small dispute at the South-West India Dock. At that time, John Burns was a comrade of William Morris and other socialists in the fractious Social Democratic Federation. Known for his agitations on behalf of the unemployed, he was soon marching through East London and into the City of London at the head of tens of thousands of striking dockers. William Morris would recover the memory of the Peasants' Revolt in his *A Dream of John Ball*, and now here were the dockers, marching in more disciplined fashion, but consciously following in the footsteps of those fourteenth-century rebels.

Their march became a daily procession throughout the strike. Burns was conspicuous with his black beard and white straw hat. As for the banners carried by the striking dockers, some were said to have been no more than red rags on poles, others consisted of 'stinking onions, old fish-heads, and indescribable pieces of meat stuck on spikes, to show the City magnates what the dockers had to live on'.

Named the strike for the 'Docker's Tanner' on account of the workers' demand for a wage of sixpence an hour, the strike 'set the movement of the unskilled aflame throughout the country'. Burns had plenty of images to hurl back at those who denounced the dockers as 'loafers' or degenerate criminals: 'I have been in the thick of starving men, with hundreds of pounds about me (they knowing it), and not a penny have I lost. I have sent men whom I did not know, for change of a gold piece, and have never been cheated of a penny. Not a man through all the weeks of that desperate Strike ever asked me for drink money…'

The strike would soon have crumbled for want of money, but Burns, Tillett and Tom Mann projected their cause as a battle for humanity rather than narrow political gain, and it was sustained by donations from fellow dockers from as far away as Australia, football clubs, the Salvation Army, and the Roman Catholic Church as represented by Cardinal Manning. The strike for the 'Docker's Tanner' was said to have been 'accompanied with a moral lift which kindled sympathy throughout the English world'. And Burns, who went on to become a Liberal Cabinet Minister, was seen as its moral dynamo as well as its megaphone. In the words of Ben Tillett:

> He used his great voice to good effect in the early days of the Strike, when he marched with other demonstrators round the docks and, standing on the backs of those who accompanied him, peered over the walls of the gates which barred his entry to Company's premises, denounced the men who remained at work, and summoned them to join the Strike in a voice of thunder. He had the instincts and the qualities of a born showman…He touched the imagination and imported humour and good temper into the Press Conferences…[13]

The dockers got their demanded sixpence an hour, and their victory greatly boosted unionization in the London docks. In a single year 200,000 dockers are said to have joined the Docks, Wharf, Riverside and General Labourer's Union of Great Britain and, for the first time, unskilled trade unionism came into membership of the TUC.

Something of the respect in which the dockers were held after 1889 can be heard in the voice of an American visitor. Mark Twain, the great novelist of the Mississippi, landed at Tilbury on Sunday, 23 June 1907, an elderly and distinguished author on his way upriver to Oxford where he would receive an honorary degree. It is not clear whether he was wearing his famous white suit, but the writer who had done so much to establish that there was history as well as mud in the Mississippi recorded his impression of the dockers who greeted him at Tilbury. Speaking to his literary friends and acquaintances at the Savage Club in London, he recalled how, on stepping ashore at Tilbury, he had received

> a good and hearty welcome from the men who do the heavy labour in the world, and save you and me having to do it. They are the men who with their hands build empires and make them prosper. It is because of them that the others are wealthy and can live in luxury. They received me with a 'Hurrah' that went to my heart. They are the men that build civilization, and without them no civilization can be built.

There were two rivers flowing through the docks of London's east river. One was the actual Thames in which dockers occasionally drowned. The other, which was surely the real 'liquid history' that John Burns had in mind, was a river of progress and solidarity surging through the hearts and minds of generations of militants and activists. It was the unstoppable river of history as sanctioned by Marx and other prophets of the Socialist Revolution. And it flowed towards a New Age that William Morris, writing *News from Nowhere* shortly after the 1889 strike, had imagined being inaugurated by a benign revolution in 1952.

Sadly the new world didn't dawn that year, but the socialist river flowed on to swell the pages of *Rising Tide*, a partisan novel written by the Australian-born classicist and Marxist Jack Lindsay and published in 1953. Based on close observation of two actual disputes, this was a dockland drama of strikes, lock-outs and international brotherhood, powered by a yearning for the working class to sail on into a socialist future in which their hunger for Art and Beauty would finally be satisfied – despite the bosses, the Labour Party and the official trade union leadership, which did everything they could to disperse the tide by exploiting 'every element of division that class-society has created among the workers'.[14]

Disappointments were many, but that idealized river of socialist aspiration was also memorialized in *Good Morning Brothers!*, the 1969 autobiography of Jack Dash, an unbridled Communist militant who led the dockers through the disputes of the sixties, and who still believed that 'When the men are determined to smash Tory policies then nothing can stop them'.[15]

For Dash, the strike of 1889 was among the great moments in a history of struggle carried out not just for the sake of better wages, but 'to uphold the principles of trade unionism, international brotherhood'. So, too, was the illicit action taken in 1919–20, when the Russian Revolution was threatened by a British government bent on sending arms and other aid to White Russian forces, or to the anti-Communist government of Poland. The left-wing *Daily Herald* printed the name of every ship departing for Poland; and the London dockers, who had organized to search the quaysides for boats shipping munitions to Poland, took their own steps against a guilty vessel called *Jolly George*, loading her in a manner that produced such a list that it was impossible to move her even within the dock.

From there, the river of socialist progress ran on through the General Strike of 1926 to make further gains under the Dock Labour Scheme introduced by the post-war Labour government of Clement Attlee. It flowed through one dispute after another into the sixties, when dock unions first won a wage increase by threatening a withdrawal of labour, and when there were further stoppages in solidarity with the under-paid nurses. John Burns's war against casual employment in the docks was now pressed towards the final goal as expressed in 'The New Dockers' Charter': a socialist Britain and a nationalized docks industry under workers' control. Nothing short of a revolution would bring this about – so thought Dash and his comrades on the 'unofficial committee' that made much of the running in those years of bitter struggle.

The Thames's militant dockers may have gone along with the crude Communist certainties of their leaders, but they were also defiantly patriotic (as Jack Dash puts it, 'it is amazing what meaning you can put into such songs as "Rule Britannia", "Sons of the Sea", and "Land of Hope and Glory" if you are in the right combative mood'). The outlook reflected East London's admirable tradition of militant self-education, of striding into the public libraries set up by philanthropists such as John Pasmore Edwards, and raising yourself with the help of books like Thomas Paine's *Age of Reason*, William Morris's *News from Nowhere*, Upton Sinclair's proletarian novel of the Chicago stockyards, *The*

Jungle, or Steinbeck's *The Grapes of Wrath*. 'Read and learn the history of the Labour movement,' that was Jack Dash's message to the young. The resilience of this riverside culture was amply demonstrated in 1970, when Ted Johns, a former wharfinger who had grown up on his grandparents' memories of the 1889 strike, was elected 'President' of the self-declared independent 'Republic' of the Isle of Dogs.

The dockers had their own downriver stories. One saga remembered by Jack Dash derived from the freakishly cold winter of 1947, when fires were burned under the quayside cranes to keep them from freezing, and a group of London dockers came across a hamper in the hold of a ship from Latin America. It was addressed to the Rt. Hon. Ernest Bevin, Foreign Secretary. Knowing very well that 'our Ernie' had once been General Secretary of the Transport & General Workers' Union, and that the word 'Brother' had meant a lot to him, the dockers moved their find to the wing of the ship's hold, and then opened

Jack Dash talking to dockers suspended after taking unofficial strike action, 10 February 1969.

it to discover a veritable feast of tinned turkey and ham, bottles of wine, cartons of cigarettes and cigars, all accompanied by a Christmas greeting from the foreign government concerned. Having improvised a table made of a packing case covered with pages from the *Daily Herald* and the *Daily Worker*, they sat down and enjoyed 'a feast equal in splendour to that of Belshazzar'. They then put the turkey carcass back in the hamper, along with the empty bottles and cigarette cartons, and sent it on its way, but not before including their own improvised Christmas card: 'Dear Ernie, wishing you a Merry Christmas, from Some of Your Own'.

If the story of the London docks and their struggles belongs in the estuary, this is partly because they themselves moved downstream over the course of the nineteenth century. The only docks still working on the Thames nowadays are at Tilbury. Constructed by the combined East and West India Dock company on 450 acres of marshland next to an isolated railway station, they were opened in 1888 in an effort to intercept the trade then going upstream to the Port of London. These vast new docks proved too remote at first, and their initial failure brought down the East and West India Dock Company. Joseph Conrad remembered them in the early years:

> Nothing in those days could have been more striking than the vast, empty basins, surrounded by miles of bare quays and the ranges of cargo-sheds, where two or three ships seemed lost like bewitched children in a forest of gaunt, hydraulic cranes. One received a wonderful impression of utter abandonment, of wasted efficiency.

But even then, half a century before containerization, it was possible to predict that 'a great future lies before Tilbury Docks'.

Statistics issued by the Port of London Authority report a healthy growth in activity over recent years, but it wasn't exactly a flowering that I saw when I visited the quayside at Tilbury Docks. Business may be booming, but the aspirations of the Great Dock Strike of 1889 seem as remote as those of Boudicca or the Peasants' Revolt.

Opposite **Loading bags of sugar on a barge, West India Docks, April 1940.**

On my visit I met John Whaley, a man who remembered the old dockers' ordeal. He once had to unload a ship that had arrived from Africa full of maggot-ridden animal remains: unimaginably disgusting stuff, perhaps destined for a glue factory, that had to be gathered into nets and then lifted ashore. Having completed the job, Whaley and his fellows were covered from head to foot in the most vile-smelling slime. But they had to ask for something to clean themselves with, and, even then, were only given a single bucket of cold water and a sponge.

Of course, there had been perks in that age of smouldering class warfare. Dockers in those days were called 'wonder boys', because of their habit of looking at crates and bundles and 'wondering what's in that'. It was said that a docker only needed to take some bread to the docks for lunch, since 'there was always something to fill a sandwich with'. But these were tiny gains and hardly sufficient to offset what another elderly ex-docker, Jim Venton, recalled as the brutality of the ship-owners, who apparently thought nothing of exposing workers to extreme and unnecessary danger.

As a participant in the disputes of the sixties and seventies, Venton wanted to make it quite clear that it wasn't industrial militancy or the dockers' working practices that put an end to the London docks, but containerization, which brought in bigger ships that could be handled by the older upright docks, and also the rise in land values, which made closure an ever more attractive option. The West India Dock ran its biggest tonnage in 1968. But the last ship, the *Blackwatch*, left the Isle of Dogs in 1983. The Port of London Authority may have turned itself into a property developer, but the dockers were stranded as the socialist river finally dried up all around them — left with memories, and a lasting hatred for Margaret Thatcher who presided over their final defeat.

No trade unions are even recognized in negotiations or bargaining at Tilbury Docks nowadays. After I had talked with John Whaley at 32 Berth, a younger docker, who had been unloading a Russian ship in the background, drove up in his fork-lift truck and denounced the 'bunch of ****s' who now own Tilbury. He insisted that 'Forth Ports', as the hated employer is now called, had even gone back to hiring temporary workers through an agency. He told me that he himself was among those who had been made redundant, and then later rehired

– with the inevitable reduction in income – through the contract labour system. 'A few people round here may not know it,' he said, 'but they've all been thrown on the rubbish tip.' It's a brutal end. A world was lost, a political tradition was cancelled, and precious few tributes were paid.

SKIPPER'S TALK

John Potter is the owner and captain of the *Princess Pocahontas*, a 180-ton tour-boat working out of Gravesend, and certainly not a traditional Thames cruiser. Indeed, despite some recent applications of paint, *Princess Pocahontas*'s stern reveals that, in a previous life, she was the *Laboe*, a river-bus from Kiel. John Potter now runs her as the first passenger ship to be based in Gravesend for twenty years and, as he proudly claims, the only one operating from east of the Thames Barrier.

Apart from acquiring his ship and satisfying the authorities that he is fit to run cruises, Potter has also had to work up his commentary. Sometimes called a 'spiel' nowadays, the river commentary is the pre-eminent organic art-form of the tidal Thames and, as Potter knows, it only has real authority if it is delivered by the skipper.

With many of its choicest observations and insults inherited from oral tradition, a good commentary draws on what the writer Joseph Addison, who frequented the London river in the early eighteenth century, once described as the 'honest prejudices which naturally cleave to the Heart of a true Englishman'.[16] In our time, this is to say that it mixes genuine practical knowledge with rumour, poetic licence and often a considerable measure of ignorant speculation, too. A colourful amalgam, it is both a burlesque and a lament for the working river: at once a stiff history-lesson imposed on an unsuspecting but captive audience of landed amnesiacs, and a series of acid put-downs directed against the new powers that have colonized the riverside and ripped its heart out. As a tirade against the world that has put so many watermen and dockers out of business, a good river-boat commentary is at least partly an act of Thames class war, too.

The average London commentary may extend from Westminster to

Greenwich, but John Potter sniffs derisively at the thought of that, and then claims to have the longest one on the river. He can start at Whitstable or Canvey Island, cruise up through the Thames Barrier and still be holding forth when he reaches Hammersmith or Kew.

The estuary being what it is, ugliness is one of his primary themes. 'If the world needed an enema, there's the place you would put the pipes.' That line is

A crane lifting a 67-ton gun at the Woolwich Arsenal, c. 1919.

reserved for Grays, a town which does indeed seem to have turned its backside on the river and sloped off over the hill, leaving only some dreary estates and a few tower-blocks to guard the old lightship that lies aslant and rotting on its forsaken pleasure beach. There's a lot of redundancy to point out, too — be it Ingress Abbey, the old Merchant Navy College, or the vast hulk of the Royal Arsenal in Woolwich, recently sold to English Partnerships for £1 and now being prepared for con-version to loft-living and other leisurely or industrial uses.

Remembering the teeming and industrious river on which he started out as a trainee waterman with Tate & Lyle, Potter declares that sailing up towards the barrier nowadays is 'like driving through a cemetery — unfortunately, it's dead'.

Fogs are familiar enough, but John Potter also has to cut his way through the billowing clouds of improving upriver rhetoric that drift downstream from the renovated Docklands area. He thinks nothing of negotiating his way past gar-gantuan container ships, but has to struggle to avoid woolly and all-embracing phrases like 'East Thames Corridor' and 'Thames Gateway' as they come blowing down on the tide, along with the government promise to bring new life to the estuary in the year 2000. 'That's the biggest load of shit,' says Potter disgustedly, adding that by selling off so many of the docks and other key sites along the old working river, they've already 'made London into a large housing estate'.

DAGENHAM TO THE BARRIER:
Triumph of the Engineers

Yet there is still grandeur amongst all the dereliction, and it may be the sea-wall rather than the docks that provides the necessary clue to its greatest tradition. For Samuel Smiles, the nineteenth-century historian of the Industrial Revolution, England's greatness was the work of her engineers. He saw the art of embanking and draining marshland as an ancient heritage that extended all the way back into antiquity – past the Romans to the 'adventurous tribes of Belgium and Friesland', who had colonized southern England by a process of 'simple persevering industry rather than of war'.[17] According to Smiles, it was these ancient colonists who had been responsible for the initial embankment of the 'great highway between the capital of Britain and the world'.

By the 1860s, when Smiles published his *Lives of the Engineers*, the Thames was 'an artificial river almost from Richmond to the sea'; and keeping it within its engineered channel had been an epic struggle, too. The Anglo-Saxon Chronicle of 1099 records flooding in the capital, and in 1236, it is said to have been possible to row boats in Westminster Hall. 'Bustings of the bank' were frequent on the southern shore between London Bridge and Greenwich. Bermondsey was often flooded, and the Combe marshes, east of Greenwich, were only won back thanks to an Italian engineer called Acontius, who received 600 acres of rescued land as his reward. The north shore was just as liable to inundation. The sixteenth century saw frequent breaches at Wapping and Limehouse, and also downriver in Essex, at Barking and Thurrock. In December 1663, Pepys records 'all White Hall having been drowned'; but worse happened when the river broke through at Limehouse in 1676, pouring over the northern end of the Isle of Dogs, following the line that would later become the West India Docks, and threatening to leave the Royal dockyard stranded high and dry at Deptford.

According to Smiles, the most 'destructive and obstinate' of these collapses occurred by a creek that joined the river near the village of Dagenham. An earlier breach here had been stopped by Cornelius Vermuyden, a Dutchman who drained the East Anglian fens and may have worked on Canvey Island, too. He had embanked Dagenham creek in 1621, but the sluices he installed were neglected, and in 1707, an inland flood coincided with a high spring tide, which broke through the sluice submerging more than a thousand acres of land and eventually creating a breach that was over 100 feet across and 30 feet deep at low tide. As the soil got washed out, a huge mud-bank built up seriously interrupting navigation over half the river.

The landowners made various attempts to fill the breach, filling old ships with chalk and stones and sinking them into the hole, followed by baskets of similar material and then bundles of straw and hay intended to deal with the remaining gaps. But the rising tide was unimpeded by such obstacles, and merely 'washed them away like so many chips'. So they tried again, this time employing 'gigantic trunks' filled with chalk and other ballast. But the tide remained unimpressed. Indeed, Smiles records that it lifted one of these 'monster trunks' from the bottom, turned and emptied it, and then carried it off downstream. A concerned landowner is said to have run along the bank shouting, 'Stop her! Oh stop her!', 'but the unwieldy object being under no guidance was carried down stream towards the shipping lying at Gravesend, where its unusual appearance, standing so high out of the water, excited great alarm amongst the sailors'.

These endeavours made no difference at all. Indeed, they encouraged scouring, which only made the breach deeper, and for years to come 'the engineering skill of England seemed likely to be completely baffled by this hole in a river's bank'. The breach had been open for seven years by 1714, when an Act of Parliament ruled that it could be closed at public expense. The job was eventually taken over by a Gloucestershire man called Captain John Perry, a former sea captain and naval officer who had recently returned from Russia where he had been variously engaged by Czar Peter, forming a royal fleet, building a canal between the rivers Don and Volga, and constructing a Royal Dockyard on the Don. Having fled Russia (he had reputedly not been paid once during his fourteen years there) Captain Perry set about the Dagenham Breach with the help of some 300 labourers.

He started by creating two subsidiary sluiced openings in the bank near the breach. Having reduced the water pressure by this means, he then set about closing the main breach gradually, by driving vast timber piles down into the riverbed, dovetailing one into the next as he went, and pouring large quantities of clay into the water outside them. The project is said to have taken five years, and to have been attended by many accidents. The water pressure intensified as the pile-drivers advanced, but the last pile finally stopped the cascade, and a vast clay bank was heaped up outside it. The 'famous breach' was finally closed. Daniel Defoe, who passed by a few years later, was pleased to be assured that 'the new work, where the breach was, is by much esteemed the strongest of all the sea walls in that level'.[18]

I couldn't spot the site of Captain Perry's heroic labours from the river, but I was reluctant to pass upstream without seeing it. So, having spent the night in an incongruous Holiday Inn perched at the edge of a Dartford housing estate and yet full of American evangelists, I crossed the new Queen Elizabeth II suspension bridge, and turned on to the A13.

Such are the traffic jams on this road that the London-bound motorist has ample opportunity to study every leaf in the Rainham marshes, and to count the containers stacked up into a vast multi-coloured ziggurat to the right, a metal alp that soars high into the sky and looks luminous as the morning sunlight plays across it. For sheer elevation, this edifice – surely one of the great sights of the A13 – is more than a match for the Beckton Ski Slope, a new amenity established on a slag heap left over by the old Beckton gas works.

After crawling along for some miles, I reached a sign asking me to choose between 'Frog Island' to the left and 'Ford Estate' to the right. Turning right, I pulled up at the Ford Heritage Centre and parked next to a bronze statue of Henry Ford. Here, I met the genial Public Affairs executive who drove me deep into a massive industrial complex which, despite major reductions in the work-force, showed little sign of dwindling in the Bata style. Eventually, we came to a small ox-bow lake in the middle of the factory, still known as the Dagenham Breach. Twenty years ago, as my guide admitted, this was seen as little more than a handy dump, but it has recently been reinstated as a pleasant landscape amenity

The Thames Barrier – designed to provide 'an icon for London' as well as to hold back the Atlantic Ocean as it surges in via the North Sea.

used by members of the Ford Angling Club. The old engine blocks have been removed and it has even been fitted with duck-houses mounted on rafts made out of old railway sleepers.

I tried to locate the precise site of Captain Perry's workings, but without success. The spot must have been close to (if not exactly under) Ford's vast and containerized jetty, and presumably also adjacent to the Ford Engine Plant, a gargantuan complex enclosing an area the size of twenty-five Wembley-sized football pitches, which sits on 20,000 concrete piles driven into the former marshland. 'We've had to engineer a few solutions,' said my guide, when I asked whether the spring tides still posed a problem. He was, I think, genuinely interested to hear about Captain Perry, but the engineer he really wanted to talk about was Richard Parry-Jones, the man responsible for the Focus, the Cougar, the Ka, and also the Mondeo.

Engineering's most recent triumph over the tidal river stretches out across the river just north of Woolwich. Designed by Charles Draper, the Thames Barrier is the world's largest navigable flood barrier – a unique structure capable of allowing a ship as large as the *Ark Royal* aircraft-carrier to pass, and yet also of stopping the Atlantic ocean, or at least 50,000 tons of water per second, as it surges in towards London from the North Sea. The barrier consists of reinforced concrete piers mounted on solid chalk below the waterline. These divide the

river into four openings, each of which has a radial gate which rests on the river-bed when open, an idea which is said to have been inspired by the mechanism of an ordinary domestic gas-tap.

Now run by the Environment Agency, the Thames Barrier was developed and built under the auspices of the late Greater London Council: the opening, in May 1984, was a rare occasion which brought

'Ash and Silk Wall' by the sculptor Vong Phaophanit, in position near the Thames Barrier.

Queen Elizabeth II on to the same platform as 'Red' Ken Livingstone. Designed to provide an 'icon for London' as well as practical defence against tidal surges, the barrier has also given new form to one of the abiding distinctions in the symbolism of the Thames. Upstream the river may still be imagined as 'liquid history', attended by Royalty and regattas and a leafy rhetoric of 'vision' and national renewal. Below the barrier, it remains less predictable in its compact with the sea – a disillusioning thing of mud and danger, a site of disconnected hulks and ruins, and of endless struggle for a working afterlife. These distinctions are older than the barrier, but they are brought into a new focus by its existence. Stand here, and look out across the river, and you can see that the Thames actually flows in from two sources – the physical one may lie upstream, but the economic, cultural and historical one surely lies in the sea, which has determined so much of what the country has become.

Considering the symbolic status of the Thames Barrier, it is appropriate that it should have found some artistic testimony over its first decade. The usual mediocre corporate video may be seen at the visitors' centre, and there is also a mural mapping the route of the new Thames path, which extends upstream, but definitely not down, from here. Yet the bravest tribute was a piece of public art called 'Ash and Silk Wall', by the sculptor Vong Phaophanit, which once stood in a landscaped park a few hundred metres south of the Thames Barrier. Commissioned in 1992 by the Public Art Development Trust, it was a strong and conceptually coherent piece of work, yet like Fobbing's memorial to the Peasants' Revolt, it failed to meet with the approval of the local art critics. By August 1995, when I went to look at it, its shattered pink remains were on the point of being carried away.

As Vong Phaophanit informed me, the site was 'partly derelict and pretty run down', and 'I knew from the beginning that it would be a problem.' The trees planted in the initial landscaping had been damaged before he began, but this made him all the more ambitious. The project was 'very challenging', but he was reluctant to accept that 'art should not be in a bad area', or that it should just be 'about making people happy'.

Ash Wall was 14 metres long, 4.5 metres tall and about 1 metre thick. A section of about 2 metres had been cut out and moved back to form 'a gateway' which was not directly visible from all angles, but could be walked through none the less. The work would gleam like the Thames Barrier itself and, since the river had long been a route of migration, trade and colonization, it would also evoke the idea of a frontier that was at once real and illusory. Vong Phaophanit chose glass for his work of art because he wanted to 'reflect' the area – catching the cars, warehouses, and the nearby wrecking yards, too. Behind the laminated glass panels, he placed salmon-pink silk on one side, and wood ash on the other. He chose these materials because he knew they meant very different things to people from 'different educational and cultural backgrounds'. He hoped that his sculpture would prompt people to reflect on the way they themselves thought about things; and to question whether an area like this part of Woolwich need always be 'a depository for unwanted objects'.

Peter Palumbo, then chairman of the Arts Council of Great Britain, came to the inauguration in September 1993, and spoke proudly of what public art could do to a formerly wasted place like this. And then, like a brave beachhead marine in the service of Culture and Urban Uplift, the work was left to fend for itself.

Ash Wall was not entirely without resources. It was internally lit, so that it would glow at night. Its glass was laminated and designed to withstand the toughest of blows. An internal alarm had been installed, and the work was supposedly also in view of the Thames Barrier's surveillance cameras. But these defences proved insufficient. First, the glass panels leaked, so that the ash darkened in places, and then the estuarial vigilantes moved in on this stranded symbol of 'regeneration'. To begin with, one or two panels of glass were smashed with stones. Then the work was rammed with huge concrete bollards, and it became routine to find rebounded rocks all around it. As Vong told me ruefully, Ash Wall turned out to be 'perfect for this kind of target practice'.

Two years later, it had been horribly defeated. Every one of its panels had been shattered, and the rocks were still piling up despite the high fence that now surrounded the injured work. The wreckage was removed soon afterwards.

DRY AS A BONE

Range all thy swannes, faire Thames, together on a ranke,
And place them duly one by one upon thy stately banke...

That was one of the easier symbolic manoeuvres that the sixteenth-century poet Michael Drayton imagined the Thames performing in tribute to its Virgin Queen.[1]

Elizabeth I's progresses took her upstream as well as down, into a wooded country of courtly masques and recitations: a pastoral Thames-side which poets, sincere or sycophantic, had planted with numerous devices besides those feathery swans. The Greek god Pan, diverse shepherdesses and a sprightly 'wild man' were waiting to jump out at her when she visited the Lady Russels at Bisham Abbey, an estate on the south bank opposite Marlow where the England football team now trains; and she endured days of flowery Latin presentations on her equally ornamented visits to Oxford.

Elizabeth I was fond of the river: so much so that she is said, while on her way to Cirencester in 1592, to have had herself carried upstream so that she could examine 'the very first trickle of my fine Thames'.[2] Precise details of that rumoured journey are not forthcoming, but we do know what the river poets thought she should find.[3] William Camden had imagined a grotto-like cave set with ivory, British jet and pumice-stone, where the Thames streamed forth in 'common brotherhood' with other great rivers of the world, the Nile, Ganges, Amazon and Rhine. Elizabethan poets, such as Edmund Spenser and Michael Drayton, persisted in the same mode, adding water nymphs, dryads and windy 'Zephyrs' to the 'verdant, flow'ry meads' of this already fleecy scene.

That poetic idea of the source would influence perceptions for centuries to come. 'Sweet Thames' was still flowing softly in the 1850s, when Mr and Mrs S.C. Hall came along to inspect its upper reaches. Guided to the leafy spot by an

Previous pages
Didcot Power Station dominates the landscape between Oxford and Abingdon, and uses Thames water for cooling purposes.

appropriately ancient shepherd, the authors of *The Book of the Thames: from its Rise to its Fall* were pleased to discover that 'the cradle of the Thames' was still 'a perfect solitude'. The sequestered nook may no longer have been studded with jewels, but it still suggested only 'contentment, parent of delight'. The Arcadian strain was sounded again in the Second World War, when the writer and engraver Robert Gibbings came by for his book *Sweet Thames Flow Softly*, and imagined Roman water-bearers coming down to the well from their nearby camp.

By then, however, the Elizabethan pastorale was much faded and the source of England's longest river was already more likely to be attended by tedious parliamentary bickering than by nymphs and dryads. The guidebooks of our time record bantering argument in the House of Commons in February 1937, when the Member for Stroud, Mr Perkins, asked that the Ordnance Survey maps should recognize a place called Seven Springs, which lies south of Cheltenham at the head of the river Churn, as the true source of the Thames. His suggestion did not impress Mr W.S. Morrison, Minister for Agriculture and MP for Cirencester and Tewkesbury, who replied that, even though the acknowledged source at Thames Head, a few miles southwest of Cirencester, did indeed sometimes dry up as Mr Perkins had claimed, 'that does not alter my view that the river Thames rises in my constituency'. Other members merely yawned, and muttered that it was Mr Perkins who should dry up.

To get to the officially acknowledged source of the Thames, you take the A429 south from Cirencester, park near a railway bridge and then walk back along the road to a gate. The source lies across a couple of flat fields in Trewsbury Mead, below the raised and wooded bank of the long disused Severn and Thames Canal, some half-a-mile from the road. A huge ash stands next to it, wind-blasted and stricken as well as venerable, although I could find no trace of the letters TH, standing for 'Thames Head', said to be carved in its bark.

There was no trace either of the statue that used to be here, a cement rendition of old Father Thames made by Rafaelle Monti in 1854. Initially, this bearded and reclining giant had adorned Crystal Palace. Sold after the fire there, it spent some years as a garden ornament before being acquired by Mr Scott Freeman, a Thames Conservator, and was eventually placed at the official source

The official and often dry source of the Thames in Trewsbury Mead, Gloucestershire.

in 1958. This monument can be seen in photographs from that time, squeezed, like some wild animal, into a cage of sturdy iron railings. But public art is apparently no safer in the Cotswolds than at the Thames Barrier, and, in 1974, it was judged prudent to shift the battered thing to a less remote location downstream.

In 1794 there was a well at Thames Head, surrounded by a stone wall, but all that remains nowadays is a rough collection of stones on the ground. A still puddle of water covers them in the winter, when the surrounding land is often flooded, but the source is often dry in the summer, and the winding line of the river only detectable as the slightest dip in the meadow.

This desiccation has prompted many disappointed responses over the years. In an attempt to animate the scene, the authors of one of the best post-war guides to the upper Thames brought in an elderly water-diviner, Mr John Sawyer, who set to work with the help of whalebone rods and sticking plaster.[4] Mr Sawyer's findings were somewhat encouraging, but he was exceptional in this respect. For generations now, Thames writers have been drawing up short

A pump at Thames Head, *c.* 1890: a more innocent machine than those that have been blamed for the dry condition of the river.

to lament the dryness of the source — unable to resist taking it as the sign of an alarming dehydration in the national bloodstream. So it was with Fred Thacker, the pre-eminent historian of the Thames, who came here in the exceptionally dry summer of 1906: 'All you get in arid seasons is an infrequent pool of still and not always sweet water. One's first emotion is almost to tears'.[5]

Searching round for something to blame for this dereliction, Thacker directed his 'absurd anger' at an 'infernal engine sucking away at the streams of the springs that should send a pleasant rivulet coursing herealong!' For him, as for many more local objectors before him, the guilty machine in the garden was the Thames and Severn Canal pumping station — 'an ungainly structure, which the lover of the picturesque may well wish away'.[6] Situated half-a-mile or so downstream from the source and since converted into a house, this apparatus was built in the late eighteenth century, powered by wind at first and equipped with a steam-engine in 1794. It drew water out of underground springs, lifting it over twenty metres, and transferred it into the always leaky canal nearby. A few years after Thacker deplored it, the mechanical despoiler had transformed into 'the Kemble pump', which provided drinking water for Swindon and was said by another regretful chronicler, Alfred Williams, to be abstracting 3 or 4 million gallons a day.[7]

Whatever the crimes of that long defunct pump, the source of the Thames (or the Isis as the river above Dorchester is sometimes still called) has actually been disappointing summer visitors for centuries. It was dry in the sixteenth century, when John Leland, who was both Henry VIII's antiquary and the Thames's first river poet, observed that 'Wher as the very Hed of Ifis ys in a great Somer Drought apperith very litle or no Water'. But if Fred Thacker wasn't the first to be reluctant to place the blame for this dryness on Nature herself, his trials were by no means over. Thirsty as well as tearful, he turned back from the source and walked to the nearby village of Kemble, only to find that it was dry, too. A few years later, Alfred Williams attributed this dismal fact to a native form of quality control, saying that the last inn in the village had been kept by a certain 'Damper' Adams, whose ale was so dire that 'a gang of men set upon the house, rolled out the casks, smashed in the heads, and sent the beer tumbling down the hill into the river.' But Thacker blamed a late and over-pious lady of the manor, claiming that she had made it a condition of her will that there would be no alcohol in the village. A dry river and a dry village: the 'stripling Thames' was shaping up as an Englishman's nightmare within its first mile.

EWEN TO LECHLADE: In the Tracks of Cornelius Uzzle

Yet despite these grave allegorical lapses at the source, the old guidebooks I consulted before setting off downstream still managed to portray the first fifteen or so miles of the Thames as an ancient and self-sufficient world that had persisted miraculously unchanged through vast tracts of English history. The 'stripling Thames' had seen the encounter of the Romans with the Dobunni, a non-Belgic tribe whose primary relic, still one of the defining features of the higher Thames landscape, is the White Horse carved into the chalk hillside at Uffington. Having formed the border between the Saxon kingdoms of Wessex and Mercia, the river had also served King Alfred as a fortified frontier against the marauding Danes.

By the Norman Conquest of 1066, the Upper Thames was, so I read, 'the most settled and civilised part of England'.[8] And it was thought to have gone its own way more or less undisturbed until the early twentieth century, when the First World War decimated the villages and the motor-car started to shrink the distances on which the survival of this innermost stretch of England had depended. Writing on the brink of the First World War, Alfred Williams portrayed the life of the Upper Thames Valley as a natural outgrowth of the river:

> Everything about the valley – pasture, tillage and crops, veg-
> etation, birds and animals, the keeping of flocks and herds,
> work, business, pleasure, recreation, the whole of life in fact,
> is governed by the river, that operates in a hundred ways,
> openly and secretly, determining all things, and whose
> decrees are absolute and irrevocable.

In these Victorian and Edwardian accounts, everything about the upper Thames valley reverberates with ancient echoes. The earliest ancestors had lived on raw fish from the river, and chewed on the roots of bulrushes. These pri-mordial types eventually gave way to hunters, who slept in the trees, with their goat horns and heavy clubs. Even in 1914, it was still thought possible that the memory of these prototypical English folk lived on in the local custom of making an annual acorn pie.

The people of the uppermost Thames had their own organic industries, like candle-making, saddlery, straw-plaiting and also glove-making which was long an important trade along the river between Cricklade and the source. There was innate wisdom in the fields, too; and Alfred Williams, who also collected the folk songs of the Upper Thames, was careful to preserve the pre-Darwinian thoughts of some haymakers he came across near Cricklade:

> For the physical features of the earth and the fossil remains
> discovered in the quarries, and ofttimes built into the walls of

their houses, they hold Noah's Flood responsible. They believe that stones and minerals grow, and affirm that the sarsens in the meadow get visibly bigger year by year: some of them, they say, are as large again as when they were boys. They are, moreover, positive that bones grow when they are buried in the earth, and that the skeleton of a man or animal will ultimately be enlarged to very much more than its original size.

Intrigued to see what trace I could find of this detonated old world seventy years later, I set off in the early summer, avoiding Kemble and not finding anything too depressing about the dry condition of the first half-mile.

The Thames from Mill Farm, Ewen, where elderly locals still talk about 'the coming of the river'.

Pools of sour and stagnant water were appearing in the river-bed by the time I arrived at Ewen. Mill Farm, a stone building standing among modern barns,

was once known as the highest mill on the Thames. When Mr and Mrs Hall came here in the 1850s, they found a jovial miller, whose only complaint was that the 'engine of the canal frequently left him without water to move his wheel'. There is no sign of that wheel now; and David Horlick, the farm manager, told me he could hardly believe there had ever been enough water to run such a device. The stream can be dry for most of the year, although it can also fill very suddenly, and at those moments the local elders still talk about 'the coming' of the river.

'No spot on the Thames is more beautiful,' says Williams of Ewen, adding that this attractive stone village was a healthy place, too – full of centenarians with hearty appetites. Cornelius Uzzle, one of these ethnic elders, is said to have devoured 12 pounds of bacon for the sake of a bet – 6 pounds raw and 6 pounds parboiled – all at single sitting in The Wild Duck Inn.

A sixteenth-century stone building, The Wild Duck remains the first pub on the river, even if Mr Uzzle and his friends have moved on. On a summer

'The Wild Duck' at Ewen, the first pub on the Thames.

weekend nowadays, the car park is likely to be full of gleaming off-road vehicles and a few Porsches, too. The publican has introduced his own version of Thameside burlesque, a gently self-mocking style that is commonly encountered on the upper river nowadays. A self-consciously classical looking sculpture of a naked swain adorns the lawn, and it is only on second glance that this apparently Arcadian fellow turns out to be examining a verruca on the sole of his foot. The entrance is ablaze with stickers, identifying this free house with upmarket weekend breaks; and both the food and the décor have been improved since Cornelius Uzzle's day. Dried hops hang overhead and there is a mad collection of wildlife on the wall: the head of a gazelle-like creature with corkscrewed horns, and a large encased eel caught in a nearby gravel pit. Among these cod-rustic trophies hangs a portrait of Diana, Princess of Wales, looking radiant at the time of her marriage. Charles hangs opposite, ceremonially clad but less honoured in display. Indeed, he is suspended just below two stuffed fishheads, which gaze out into the bar in open-jawed amazement.

Further on, I passed through the flooded gravel pits now serving as the Cotswold Water Park to Ashton Keynes, where the Thames is a bright stream running alongside the main street and serving as a moat to its well-appointed houses. A painting of the 'Baby Thames' here may have been reproduced as a frontispiece in *The Old Country*,[9] a patriotic anthology of poetry and prose published during the First World War, but a more recent traveller has objected that 'the design of many of the bridges is undistinguished'.[10] There are a few reminders that rural poverty still exists among the commuters, but you could do worse than cite Ashton Keynes if you wanted to argue that Cotswold limestone is an upwardly mobile building material. Concern about the river's tendency to run dry persists. I heard mutterings about water extraction, and the place bristles with accusing fingers pointed at the local pumping station, at the gravel extractors at the nearby Cotswold Water Park, and at Swindon, a large and far from traditional conurbation to the south-east.

Cricklade is the first town on the Thames. King Alfred fortified the place against the Danes and it is said that violence was still breaking out in the pubs here at the beginning of the twentieth century, thanks to the local custom of asking strangers to perform an odd manoeuvre called the funnel trick. Having tucked a large funnel into the front of his trousers, the victim was invited to tilt his head right back, lay a coin on the middle of his forehead and then, by repeated movements of the brows, wiggle it down his nose until it fell into the funnel. Predictably enough, while he was concentrating on this, one of the locals would pour a potful of ale into the funnel.

Nowadays, Cricklade is known for its flowering North Meadow, a hundred-acre stretch of common land on which 80 per cent of the country's fritillaries are said to grow. And yet it is also here that a harder reality cuts in. In November 1821, William Cobbett, that great breaker of pastoral visions, visited Cricklade during the course of his *Rural Rides*, and was apparently quite unaware that he was in a land of ancient rustic contentment: 'I passed through that villainous hole, Cricklade, about two hours ago; and, certainly, a more rascally looking place I never set eyes upon. I wished to avoid it but could get along no other way.' Cobbett was enraged by the contrast between the richness of Cricklade's fields and the dire poverty of those who worked them, and noted that 'no society ought to exist where the labourers live in a hog-like way'. Surrounded by fine agricultural land, Cricklade was nevertheless a place of 'deplorable want…In my whole life I never saw human wretchedness equal to this: no, not even among the free Negroes in America…'

In the absence of firewood, the miserable labourers were reduced to scurrying around in search of bean stubble with which to warm themselves. Their houses, meanwhile, were 'little better than pig-beds, and their looks indicate that their food is not nearly equal to that of a pig'. Indeed, such was the ruthlessness of the landlords that these hovels were actually stuck upon 'little bits of ground on the roadside, where the space has been wider than the road demanded'. It was, thought Cobbett, as if they had been swept up from the fields and dumped down here by a hurricane.

The cause of this dislocation was partly 'an accursed Canal', which enabled the plentiful food grown around Cricklade to be shipped off to be sold to the 'tax-eaters' in the city. It was partly 'the desolating and damnable system of paper-money' through which the rich aggregated small homesteads into larger monopolizing farms. Above all, however, Cricklade had long been famous as one of the worst 'rotten boroughs' in England, one where any rogue with enough money could be sure of bringing about their own election.

In that age before the secret ballot, elections were carried out in the aisle of the church. Votes were easily bought, and honest candidates never stood the slightest chance against the wealthy adventurers who opposed them. Several days before the election, the pubs would be flowing with free drinks, and candidates would visit voters, lending them money without security, or offering prodigious sums for their worthless old pictures or even their pet canaries. Some inhabaitants of Cricklade would even chalk the price of their vote on their doors.

In 1807, votes were said to cost as much as 45 guineas each; and one candidate in a North Wiltshire election is reputed to have sold 50 acres of good pasture just to pay for the ribbons worn by his supporters. Squire Archer of

Baptising at Cricklade.

Lushill was at the fore in Cricklade elections. Well known for the meanness of his wages, he is said to have lost three top hats on one polling day, and been chased home across the fields with the rim of one of them still hanging round his neck.

It was early evening by the time I arrived at this once notorious town. I was full of anticipation, but my enquiries did not go well. I met a fellow by the bridge who called the Thames 'a good servant' and swore that he could predict the river's fullness by the moon. But when I entered The White Lion, a harsh-voiced woman behind the bar barked 'Second on the right' with such force that I felt obliged to follow her directions. On doing so, I found myself at the Gents', an amenity which I hadn't asked for, but which I duly attended. There was unyielding silence when I mentioned the days of the rotten borough; and I decided against asking after the 'Funnel Trick' or picking up the tab for Cobbett's description of Cricklade as 'a villainous hole'.

I met with further indifference when I enquired after the whereabouts of Hatchett's Ford. Redirected across the road, I entered the post office, where the postmistress looked me up and down, and then fired me off through a little housing estate where I eventually found the place in the midst of an untidy yard known as Abingdon Court Farm.

Opposite **Cricklade's Particular Baptists conducting their last baptismal ceremony in the Thames at Hatchett's Ford.**

It was getting dark and the disused ford was deserted except for a solitary woman walking a large dog along what's left of the river bank here. Noting the arrival of a stranger, she leashed the beast, drew it in close and seemed to prepare for the worst. In a miscalculated attempt to reassure her, I explained that I had come to see the place where, into the early twentienth century, Cricklade's Particular Baptists used to gather to witness the baptism of adult members in the river. She expressed surprise and even polite interest in this unlikely fact, while all the time continuing her cautious retreat.

Had the conversation gone better, I might also have asked her if she could confirm my suspicion that Hatchett's Ford had seen the launch of another Christian crusade. It was surely here on Christmas Eve in 1966 that Alexander Wozniak, a Polish engineering draughtsman who lived at Dagenham, had launched himself on an eccentric river-trip intended to celebrate 1000 years of Christianity in Poland. With his feet planted in unorthodox contrivances called 'skinoes', and a float-ended pole clasped in each hand, he headed off for Westminster pier, fortified by lemonade and vodka.

Alexander Wozniak leaving Cricklade on his 'skinoes,' Christmas Eve 1966. He reached Westminster on New Year's Eve.

But the question was best left unasked. The river may have seemed an eternally reassuring thing to Elizabethan river-poets and Edwardian topographers alike, but I had got nowhere by appealing to the past in Cricklade. Indeed, I had only made myself seem shifty and possibly a good deal worse. As for Mr Wozniak, he only came here in order to leave as sensationally as possible, and, as I made my more modest exit, I couldn't think of much reason why the people of Cricklade should remember either of us.

Lechlade is nowadays dominated by antique shops, but it is neither they, nor the duly commemorated fact that Shelley once wrote a poem in the churchyard, that put this Gloucestershire town on the map. For many centuries now, Lechlade has been the head of navigation on the Thames. Daniel Defoe records seeing 'very large barges at the key' when he passed through in the 1720s, and, by the late eighteenth century, it was here that the Severn and Thames Canal, so loathed by Cobbett, began.

In 1677, a pirate named Captain Cutler used to operate here, at least according to the people of Cricklade who claimed that vessels were being refused passage at St John's Bridge unless they paid an illegal levy. Nowadays, however, the most prominent sign of history at St John's is the relocated cement statue of Father Thames. Brought here from the source and squeezed into place between St John's Lock and the lock-keeper's garden, it is a work that proves how successfully Victorian fancy anticipated the late twentieth-century garden-centre. Much knocked about, Father Thames reclines here, patched and repointed, as the acceptable face of public art.

Lechlade's place in the history of the working Thames can be measured in the high arch of its Halfpenny Bridge, and also in its docks, now converted into a boat-yard and a scruffy marina with tinkering men, trinket shacks, and rotten old boats hoisted ashore and turned into flower beds. The summer nowadays finds many leisure craft tied up at the bank below the bridge while their occupants busy themselves polishing brass fittings up to a high shine, replenishing the geraniums and salvias planted in cast-iron pots on the top of their cabins, or just wandering back from the supermarket with plastic bags full of provisions. I glimpsed a couple pouring gin and tonic into plastic cups, but this mixed fleet contains no examples of what one commentator has called 'the more garish kind of cocktail-bar cruiser', vessels which are just too big to get through Osney Bridge at Oxford.

This is a genial scene, and nobody would resent these summer visitors the leisure of the meandering river, let alone revile them as alien invaders from the urban civilization downstream. Yet it wasn't always like that on this reach of the upper Thames. Elizabeth I's river-poets may have looked downriver and seen London as a culminating glory, but the upstream allegorists of the Victorian age were more inclined to view the city as an industrial nightmare, a cancerous growth creeping up the river to explode deep within the heart of the nation. This is how it appeared to Richard Jefferies, a country writer of the Victorian age, who came to expect more of the Thames than that it should flow softly down to the sea.

Having grown up on his father's small subsistence farm at Coate Water, near Swindon, Jefferies worked as a reporter for the *North Wilts Herald*, but circumstances drew him out of the Vale of White Horse into London, where he lost his rural solitude to the seething industrial crowd and his health to tuberculosis. Jefferies wrote much about the rural life he had known in the valleys of the upper Thames, but the thought of London was enough to turn this sympathetic observer of country life into a catastrophist who, in his imagination at least, yearned after disaster on an apocalyptic scale.

Jefferies took his revenge on that unclean city and its industrial civilization in *After London*, a futuristic romance written in Brighton in 1884. In this book, the Thames that flowed softly for Spenser is re-imagined as a cleansing catastrophe that wipes away London and its ever-expanding suburbs. With unmistakable relish, Jefferies portrays the Thames, swollen by a great flood, sweeping away all the suburban housing along its broken banks, smashing its way through the bridges, whether of stone or iron, and then bursting up through the sewers, to suck London's buildings down into a vile stinking swamp. In the absence of any worldly agency to carry out such a hygienic transformation, Jefferies attributed it to the passage of 'an enormous dark body through space', one that tilted the earth and caused a vast volume of rain to fall.

Below Lechlade, for long the head of navigation on the Thames, seen from Inglesham Church in the 1880s.

The result was an abandoned landscape in which people as well as plants and animals had reverted to 'wild times'. There was no long-term future for the lions, tigers, bears and 'monstrous serpents' that had escaped from the zoos but the beaver had successfully naturalized. At the centre of this violently purged and reforested country is 'the Lake', a vast fresh-water ocean, 'the very mirror of purity' which stretches out from the Severn near Bristol, to Oxford and then on through the 'straits of White Horse', to the poisonous marshes covering the site of the old metropolis: 'a vast stagnant swamp, which no man dare enter, since death would be his inevitable fate'.

To walk in this toxic zone is to leave luminous phosphorescent footprints on fetid black earth 'composed of the mouldering bodies of millions of men'. It is to see the foul yellow air flaring in spontaneous combustion, and to find nothing left of the houses except for white crystalline walls that crumble on touch. This fatal swamp is 'the very essence of corruption' and, in portraying it as such, Jefferies made full use of the estuary's downriver myths of marsh fever. Here, once again, are the 'miasma', the rotten vapours and 'exhalations' which caused such concern before the link with *anopheles* mosquitoes

Father Thames, as rendered by Rafaelle Monti in 1854: now chipped and battered, but still holding out against the vandals at St John's Lock, Lechlade.

was established. As for the 'contour of death' that kept better-off people away from the marshes, that is here, too, although Jefferies has redrawn it so that the fatal 'ague or fever' will strike anyone foolish enough to dig into, or even sleep on, the ground of any former human habitation.

KELMSCOTT: Utopia with B52s

This morbid fantasy, in which urban-industrial pollution becomes the defining image of Evil, may seem more appropriate to a twentieth-century catastrophist like J.G. Ballard, whose novel of flooded London, *The Drowned World*, it predates by nearly eighty years. Yet it found its admirers along the banks of the nineteenth-century upper Thames, too. The predominantly Elizabethan house associated with the most influential of these lies just downstream from Lechlade, close to a crumbling pill-box left over from the Second World War.

Kelmscott Manor, a gabled grey-stone residence, standing in a gracious cluster of barns and dovecotes, is now a shrine dedicated to the memory of William Morris, poet, designer, visionary prophet of the Arts and Crafts movement, and also the pioneering conservationist who formed the Society for the Protection of Ancient Buildings in March 1877. It is a captivating place given over to stitches, folds, and a carefully reinstated sense of medieval measure.

I visited Kelmscott one Wednesday in June, to find it thronging with visitors, a good number of whom were themselves artfully embroidered. There was a sense of strained politeness in the air, as people tried to commune with the spirit of the Pre-Raphaelites while also queuing up at doorways and the narrow staircase leading into the once-laddered attic-rooms, and congealing into thick clusters around key exhibits: Morris's four-poster bed with its embroidered valance, say, or Janey's jewellery box, a wedding present specially decorated by Dante Gabriel Rossetti and Lizzie Siddal. I heard people talking about the weave of tapestries, and teasing out the difference between Morris's organic approach to decoration and the latter-day practice called interior design. Inevitably, there was also some speculation about the triangular passions that developed between William Morris, Dante Gabriel Rossetti and Janey Morris, the working-class 'stunner' who served as ethereal model and consort to them both.

After wandering through those busy Pre-Raphaelite rooms, I withdrew to the tea-barn and wondered about what I had just seen. There can be no doubt that Morris invested his heart in this place, even if his actual visits were rarely longer than his summer holidays. Associating Kelmscott with a 'delightful quickening of perception in which everything gets emphasised and brightened',[11] he fished gudgeon from the Thames, with the help of a punt, and found one of his best-known wallpaper designs, 'Willow Bough', in the garden. As his daughter, May Morris, remembered in 1936, 'We were walking one day by our little stream that runs into the Thames and my Father pointed out the detail and variety in the leaf forms, and soon afterwards this paper was done, a keenly observed rendering of our willows that has embowered many a London living room.'[12]

William Morris was concerned with 'making life pleasanter and more varied', but it takes a positive effort, sitting in this leafy bower, to remember that he spelt out this project not in a nineteenth-century precursor of *Country Living* magazine but in a lecture entitled 'What Socialists Want'.[13] He may have been a lover of willows but he was also a Communist and, unlike many of his late twentieth-century admirers, not at all shy of pronouncing it. That still untested nineteenth-century idea would go on to convulse whole continents, but, in England, we have managed to conserve it as a matter of craft and décor. William Morris may have imagined Kelmscott as the prefiguration of a new, post-revolutionary order. But, nowadays, it looks less like the future than the beautifully crafted holiday home it actually was.

This displacement of urban revolution into rusticated arts and crafts has had consequences downriver as well as along the banks of the upper Thames. Many East London radicals of the early twentieth century found Morris's *News from Nowhere* all the more inspiring for the fact that its envisioned future was defined against the city of their time. That is how it was received in the Stepney flat of the German anarchist Rudolf Rocker, a theorist, agitator and editor of the *Arbeiter Fraind*, a Yiddish anarchist weekly. With its medievalism and its cultivation of handicraft, Kelmscott might as well have been on another planet, and yet the Rockers and their friends drew strength from Morris's vision of a world of individual buildings and spires rather than drab tenements, factories and gas-holders.[14]

In more recent years, however, the upstream cult of Morris seems to have obscured his roots downriver. While at Kelmscott, I remembered speaking to the Jim Venton, a former docker, whom I had met at a pub called The World's End at Tilbury. Having grown up with men who had been directly involved in the Great Strike of 1889, he seemed to know everything about that dispute and

Kelmscott as drawn by William Morris for *News from Nowhere*.

the contribution of heroic leaders such as John Burns and Ben Tillett. But when I mentioned William Morris, Venton looked at me quizzically and asked, 'You mean the wallpaper designer?' Thanks to the coverage of recent years, he knew quite a lot about Morris's recovery of craft, but that very knowledge seemed to make it all the more unlikely that Morris had ever had any connection with the urban working-class struggle of his time.

As it happens, the 1889 dock strike taught Morris himself a thing or two about the dangers of spreading your hopes across the great divide between town and country. He was staying at Kelmscott for the first two weeks of the dispute, and the first notes he wrote about it for the socialist paper *Commonweal* were, in the judgement of the socialist historian E.P. Thompson, highly disappointing. Engels may have seen 'the rebirth of the English working class' in the unrest of those years but Morris, who sat sequestered among his tapestries and willows, 'sadly underestimated the event, expressing the need for a "general combination" of the workers' and emphasizing 'the necessary failure of strikes which did not, for exceptional reasons, have the backing of public opinion'. It was only later, when he returned to his London home in Hammersmith, that Morris realized the importance of the dispute 'which I had not at all understood in the country'; and even then, he was inclined to cavil over whether the strike was truly socialist or 'a mere combination amongst the men'.

The Thames may be a short river, but the perspectives change dramatically along its length, and not just in the revolutionary manner explored in Morris's utopian novel *News from Nowhere*. First published in *Commonweal* in 1890, this is the futuristic romance in which Morris envisions the socialist future as it might be in the twenty-first century. But the book is also a dreamer's journey in which the difference between Before and After is measured out along the length of the Thames between Morris's Hammersmith home and Kelmscott.

Richard Jefferies's *After London* may have confirmed Morris in his belief that only a violent paroxysm would clear the road to social justice, but the 'Great Change' that led to the renovated world of *News from Nowhere* is a revolution made by people, not a freakish inundation caused by a passing star. Morris's convulsion begins after the forces of law and order use machine-guns to massacre some 2000 demonstrators in Trafalgar Square. This outrage precipitates the outbreak of a Civil War and the emergence of a new era.

Morris's dreamer awakes in a London that has been thinned out: the banks of its river have been cleansed of industrial plants and engineering works; and the vanished slums replaced with gracious gardened habitations of red brick, timber and plaster, in which a medieval sense of scale has been restored. A 'great clearance' has stripped the monuments to 'fools and knaves' out of Westminster Abbey, and the Houses of Parliament have been converted into a manure store called 'Dung Market'.

While the city has been thinned out, the country that once consisted of 'clearings amongst the woods and wastes' has been resettled as a garden, with the population spread through it in harmonious, unshowy buildings. Trim and clean, with its historical relics properly integrated into the present, it no longer displays the decadent beauty that Morris describes as 'tumble-down picturesque'. First encountered at a market in Hammersmith, 'the people of the Thames valley' are not poor, broken creatures of the kind that Cobbett encountered in Cricklade, but handsome, healthy, full of character and appealing in every way: no more the 'mingled boredom and anxiety' which was 'the usual expression of the modern Anglo-Saxon face'.

Morris's journey upstream takes us up a cleansed river in which salmon run free and the injustices of history have been set right. Windsor Castle has been preserved for its antiquity, but it has also been purged of royalty and put to the use of the community – 'a great many people live there'. Eton College has been won back from the wealthy élite and converted into a socially useful school which retains a fine library. Gone is the 'hideous vulgarity' of the 'cockney villas of the well-to-do, stockbrokers and other such, which in older time marred the beauty of the bough-hung banks'. The bridges have also been transformed. The one at Hampton Court is 'no longer the old hideous iron abortion, but a handsome piece of very solid oak framing'. Morris's 'Nowhere' is a world without money, masters and priests, and, as its innermost landscape, 'the whole of Thames side is a park'.

'Nowhere' is partly imagined as a transformed land, a world made good by revolutionary change, but Morris's boat trip into the future is also powered by a more fanciful process of subtraction. He takes out the railway lines that had killed the working river, and the despised canal, too. He takes out centralized mismanagement along with money, and dismisses the Thames Conservators as heedless London bureaucrats who simply cut down the trees, ruining banks and indulging in unnecessary dredging, while all the time drawing a salary for 'masterly inactivity'. He removes the distinction between the 'Cockneyfied' suburban Thames and the 'deeper country under the foothills of the White Horse'. Wary of all machines, he almost strips out the locks along with the iron bridges, but eventually decides to keep them rather than risk the coming of another gimcrack invention.

Nobody in 'Nowhere' would ever close the blinds on beauty, as Morris once remembered a businessman doing so brutally as their train came out of a tunnel into the bright glories of the Chilterns. Machines have been abandoned because they could not produce works of art; and the detached and decadent world of 'fine art' has been overthrown, too, replaced with a more practical art, which restores the connection between people and things: an art that is grounded in the life of the household and community and 'a necessary part of the labour of every man who produces'.

Kelmscott is the goal at the end of Morris's river – the emblem of a liberated world in which 'the house shall be like a natural growth of the meadow, and the city a necessary fulfilment of the valley'. It is a crafty utopia set in high summer, the perfect crystallization of a romantic socialist pastorale. A little field near the house, perhaps the very one that now serves as a visitors' car park, is full of tents accommodating 'scientific men and historians, and students' who have come to help with the hay-making. Morris's Year Zero is a summer holiday: leafy and benign, a pastoral interlude in which even professors stir themselves, and don't require a ruthless totalitarian like Chairman Mao or Pol Pot to drive them out of the city or terrorize them into working in the fields.

Nowadays, Kelmscott has the slightly sad aura of a vision that has to be conserved against a history that has overtaken it. There are still rooks at Kelmscott, struggling to come to terms with the shortage of roosts caused by Dutch elm disease, and also with the vast warplanes that join their raucous circulation from the nearby airbases: Brize Norton, Benson or RAF Fairford, directly north of the Thames at Kempsford, where American B52 bombers rally in preparation for actions in Iraq or Serbia. The hated Machine has grown since Morris's time; and the Revolution that was meant to tame it has retreated into what one broadly sympathetic historian of the Arts and Crafts movement has called 'sighing among flowered chintzes'.[15]

Yet the poignancy of Kelmscott and its smartly restored image of the ancient future is not just about realizing that Morris belonged to his time rather than ours. It also reflects the defeat of the practical projects which attempted to give wider realization to the political aspects of his vision.

The fate of the nineteenth-century Arts and Crafts movement is exemplified by the story of the Guild of Handicraft formed by C.R. Ashbee. Founded in East London in the 1880s, this initiative was inspired by Morris's example; indeed, its members visited Kelmscott to pay their respects on a river trip up the Thames. Having started in Commercial Street, Whitechapel, the Guild later moved to Mile End Road, where it thrived as a flourishing co-operative enterprise, involving furniture makers, silversmiths and jewellers. But then Ashbee made his fatal mistake and decided to 'leave Babylon and go home to the land'.

A NATO jet heading for the Balkans from Fairford airbase, just north of the Thames at Kempsford.

So, in 1902 the guild moved to the Cotswold village of Chipping Campden – a relocation that involved some 150 men, women and children in all, and which revealed the countryside to be intrinsically neither virtuous nor fruitful. There was considerable tension with the locals who, not surprisingly, resented this vast urban invasion, and by 1907 the guild was in such dire financial straits that it had to be wound up. Lack of transport and communication had aggravated the difficulties of running a considerable workshop in isolation from its markets. In East London, Ashbee's guild had been able to get through lean periods by encouraging members to go off and work temporarily for other employers until the postcard came calling them back to the Guild. But no such arrangements could be made in the Cotswolds.

Such was the fate of Ashbee's attempt to found an alternative community in which handicraft would triumph over industrial production and the hated machine. Other followers of Morris tried to produce a version of Guild Socialism that would not be confined to medievalism and small-scale handicraft production. G.D.H. Cole did as much as anyone to derive a form capable of engaging with the problems of industrial production and the interests of the urban working class. Much influenced by Morris's *News from Nowhere*, which he described as 'the vision of a society in which it would be a fine and fortunate experience to live', Cole formed a National Guilds League in 1915, and pushed for new forms of participatory organization for consumers and workers, local decision-making, and a decentralized state which would consist of territorial groups – 'a multi-centred plural public power'.[16] Conceiving of industry as a service which could best be advanced by the introduction of factory councils and democratically elected managers, Cole tried to develop a 'third way' between private enterprise and the collectivized state. However, he drew hostile fire from both left and right, and his vision was a discarded anachronism by the 1930s when the tide of state intervention and centralized 'planning' started to rise.

HOBBITS IN OXFORD

If the ambitious politics of 'Nowhere' died, the other-worldliness lived on – a fact that leads us further down the river to Oxford, a town built on a gravel plateau at the junction of the Thames and the Cherwell, which Morris regarded highly for its ancient roots if not for its scholars. The priory that once stood at Christ Church is attributed to the eighth-century St Frideswide, the beautiful daughter of a Wessex king who, as legend goes, escaped abduction by a Mercian suitor called Algar, with the help of an angel who rowed her downriver to Abingdon. In the ninth century, Oxford was part of Alfred's Wessex, one of the fords he had fortified against the Danes to the north, and it had its trials in the age of Aethelred the Unready – indeed, in 1010, it was fired by Thorkell the Tall and his river-borne Danish raiders.

Christchurch Meadows, Oxford, viewed from a punt.

William Morris was scathing about the colleges which grew out of religious settlements in the thirteenth century. In *News from Nowhere*, he described them as 'the breeding places of a peculiar class of parasites, who call themselves cultivated people'. Treated as jesters by the rich middle classes, these pompous idlers were really 'the bores of society. They were laughed at, despised – and paid.'

And yet it was in this world that William Morris was to find some of his most influential inheritors. G.D.H. Cole was a reader in Economics at Oxford, but Morris's Oxford admirers included another 'small group of sympathetic souls in battle against a hostile society'.[17] Collectively known as 'The Inklings', this inter-war grouping included C.S. Lewis of Magdalene College who had admired Morris while at school, and lectured the literary society on him as a student at Oxford. Morris's medievalism, his anti-industrialism and his habit of building benign other worlds out of medieval and old Icelandic remnants inspired Lewis to create his own fantasy land in *The Lion, the Witch and the Wardrobe*, and the other *Chronicles of Narnia*.

Another member of 'The Inklings', J.R.R. Tolkien, fell under Morris's spell while a student at Exeter College, and went on to write his own fantasies, *The Lord of the Rings, The Silmarillion* and *The Hobbit*, with its river full of dwarves floating downstream in barrels. After Morris then, the dying enchantment of a world that once belonged to elves, and a hatred of technology and machines, represented by the dark land of Mordor and the terrible mechanization of Middle Earth. As Christian Tories, neither Lewis nor Tolkien had any sympathy for Morris's revolutionary politics, but they shared his hatred of 'materialism' and industry, and their anti-modern protest joined his as they 'flowed with the deeper stream of British romanticism'. Indeed, it wouldn't be long before that stream eddied back, and people were describing the Pre-Raphaelites of Kelmscott as 'hobbits without furry feet'.

Whatever the virtues of Lewis and Tolkien, their works inspired some dreadful inanity in the sixties and seventies, when Pre-Raphaelitism collapsed into joss-sticks and patchouli oil at the craft fair, and when every high street, including, no doubt, Oxford's, had a boutique called Gandalf's Garden and yearned for a psychedelic club called Middle Earth. There was a lot of infantile escapism in that late manifestation, personified by the 'stoned' pixies who used to stagger around clutching rune staffs and LPs by Tyrannosaurus Rex in the years that were actually defined by the oil crisis and the miners' strike. The Pre-Raphaelite stream may have flowed on into real ale and 'Green' protestation since the early seventies; and Morris would surely approve of the simple water-purification systems and other 'intermediate technology' developed by Oxfam since it was founded as the Oxford Committee for Famine Relief in the 1940s. But nothing will cure me of the suspicion that one of the lessons of Kelmscott and its posthumous cult should be, 'Never trust a Pre-Raphaelite.'

WILLIAM'S MECHANICAL NAMESAKE

'This is not an age of inventions.' So wrote William Morris of the Utopian future in *News from Nowhere*, as if the very idea of invention could only lead to more pollution, injustice and exploitation.

But there was another William Morris in Oxford at that time, and one who is most unlikely to have shared that sentiment. William Richard Morris was a local man, albeit one who would later deny that he had ever been known as 'Bill'.[18] In 1891, the year in which *News from Nowhere* appeared in its first English edition, this other William Morris was fourteen years old and to be found riding a penny farthing bicycle along the Garsington Road near Cowley. Caught up in the cycling craze of that decade, he was soon tinkering with a cross-framed safety bicycle, and figuring out his own improvements to its design. By 1893, a year in which William of Kelmscott visited Oxford to advise the university against a proposed 'restoration' of St Mary's Church, William of Cowley was apprenticed to a cycle dealer in St Giles, Oxford. A considerable cycle racer, he would soon be assembling and selling his own 'Morris' bicycles from a shop at 48 Oxford High Street.

But the major transformation in this second Morris's career took place after 1896, the year in which his Pre-Raphaelite namesake died and was brought back to be buried at Kelmscott by train and rustic wagon cart. His first experiments with the internal combustion engine were concerned with motor cycles – Morris registered his first design in 1902, but his company, the Oxford Automobile and Cycle Agency, was also involved in garaging and repairing cars. Leaving two-wheelers behind in 1908, Morris ran a car-hire service patronized by wealthy undergraduates, and it was with the assistance of one of the latter, the Earl of Macclesfield, that he assembled his own first model in 1912: a two-seater vehicle known as the Morris Oxford, or the 'Bullnose', which was immediately in competition with the four-seater Model T Ford.

From there, things proceeded quickly enough for this Oxfordshire garage-owner. The Great War involved a detour into grenades and bomb-casings, but in the following decade Morris emerged as a car-maker and packager to the middle classes – offering hire purchase and insurance arrangements along with his cars and becoming known for a 'philosophy', which prioritized large-scale manufacture, and relied on specialist outside companies to produce the constituent parts of his vehicles.

The story of Morris Motors is a Thames-side saga of the industrial kind, in which much is made of the introduction of front-wheel brakes, say, or of pressed-steel bodies; and in which rival manufacturers, such as Riley and Wolseley, are driven to the edge and then bought up advantageously. The first Morris Minor, a £100 car, went into production in 1929, and a new factory for the production of the MG Midget was built a few miles downriver at Abingdon the following year. Conveyorized production was introduced with the Morris Eight in 1934; and, in 1936, the company was joined by Turkish-born car designer Alex Issigonis, who started on the Morris Ten but would eventually design the new Morris Minor and also the Mini.

By 1938, William Richard Morris had become Lord Nuffield, a motor magnate, who was also a considerable philanthropist, funding programmes for the unemployed, recreational facilities for the Armed Forces, hospitals and medical, social and scientific research, latterly through the Nuffield Foundation and also Nuffield College, which he established at Oxford. It is said that shortly before he died in 1963, Lord Nuffield remarked that, while he may indeed have presided over the development of a machine that had changed the world for the worse, he had at least tried to do good with the fortune he had accumulated.

As handsome a car as you'll meet anywhere

Recognised always as a really good car, the Oxford makes even more admirers for its smart Sports Coupé model. Here you have a pleasant suggestion of fast travelling with the agreeable assurance of the Oxford's traditional soundness behind it. Although much is gained in appearance, nothing is lost in riding and driving comfort. Motorists who long for more than mere superficial smartness find an irresistible appeal in this Oxford Sports Coupé.
MORRIS MOTORS LIMITED, COWLEY, OXFORD

Morris Cars are guaranteed 2 years
PRICES, MORRIS-OXFORD "6"
2-DOOR 4-SEATER SPORTS COUPÉ   £285
2-DOOR 4-SEATER COUPÉ £275
4-DOOR SALOON   £265
Morris fit Triplex Glass throughout

MORRIS OXFORD
SPORTS COUPÉS

Breaking up the distances with the other William Morris, here advertising his Morris Oxford sports coupé, 1936.

When it came to breaking up the distances to which rustic travellers attributed the preservation of rural areas like the Upper Thames valley, there can be little doubt that the car had already done its business by the time Lord Nuffield retired in 1952, leaving others to see through the major redundancy programme that came four years later, and to continue the business of folding one car manufacturer into another.

In 1966, Morris's British Motor Corporation combined with Jaguar to form British Motor Holdings, which was in turn merged with Leyland to form British Leyland (BL) two years later. That company was nationalized when it went bankrupt in 1974, and later restructured under Michael Edwardes –

whose ruthless recovery plan was introduced in 1979. The Morris name finally slid into redundancy with the Marina, a car that went out of production in 1983.

Eventually BL disappeared into the Rover Group, bought first by British Aerospace in 1988, and then by BMW in 1994. This succession of corporate take-overs has brought an endless wave of demolition and rebuilding to Cowley. Under BMW, an entirely new factory has been built, dedicated to production of the Rover 75, which was unveiled as a car with 'soul' at the Birmingham International Motor Show on 20 October 1998, and duly noted for its heavy use of chrome, its Rover grille, its leathery interior, and for its shell, described as 'Rule Britannia circa 1955'.

Stylistically, the Rover 75 is a bundle of quotations from the Rovers of the forties and fifties, and yet, as the company press release explains, the aim was to be 'forward-looking' as well as 'quintessentially British'. So, rather than just wrapping the famously anti-industrial trappings of Englishness around superior rattle-free German technology, the designers set out to find a luxurious new synthesis between performance and character. Had they been earnestly determined to produce what the press release called a 'thoroughbred' English car, they would surely have added running-boards and lined the seats with one of the willowy chintzes designed by William Morris at Kelmscott. Since the other William Morris had already named one of his cars the 'Isis', they might even have felt obliged to call the thing the Rover Thames.

WITTENHAM CLUMPS: The Science of Nature

A different balance between technology and the historical landscape emerges as the Thames runs through Oxford and south past Abingdon. The most prominent feature in the landscape here is Wittenham Clumps, two rounded chalk hills capped with clumps of beech trees also known as Sinodun Hills, which rise behind Wittenham Wood on the southwest bank of the river opposite Dorchester. Unlike Round Hill, the clump on Castle Hill grows within the ramparts of an Iron Age hill fort built at about 500BC, and some 400 years older than the larger encampment that replaced it — a valley fort whose earthworks, known as Dyke Hills, can be seen directly across the Thames at Dorchester, a mile or so from here.

According to Eric de Maré, who explored the Thames in the years around 1950, the Wittenham Clumps were known locally as 'the Berkshire Bubs' and 'Mother Dunch's Buttocks', the latter being a reference to an owner who fell out of local favour by taking the Royalist side during the English Civil War. They were to be treated more respectfully by Paul Nash, the artist, who first visited the area with his family shortly before the First World War. As Nash once wrote: 'Ever since I remember them the clumps have meant something to me. I felt their importance long before I knew their history. They eclipsed the impression of all the early landscapes I knew… They were the Pyramids of my small world.'[19]

Sensing an 'ancient nearness' in the folds of this fortified landscape, Nash reconfigured the clumps as a magical place where every physical presence was enfolded in the palpable wonder of its own creation. He considered Wittenham 'a beautiful legendary country haunted by old gods long forgotten'. Some of his

Paul Nash's drawing, 'The Wood on the Hill,' 1912.

paintings leave little doubt that a full-breasted earth mother – perhaps a variant on Mother Dunch – was among those primitive deities, but his clumps had a 'Pan-ish enchantment', too. Nash first drew and painted these enigmatic swellings before the Great War, and he returned to them in many of the great paintings of his last years in the 1940s. In works such as 'Landscape of the Summer Solstice', 'Landscape of the Vernal Equinox' and 'Landscape of the Moon's Last Phase', he uses the clumps to suggest secret correspondences between sun and moon, or to trace cosmological symmetries between sunflower or dandelion and sun.

Nowadays, the clumps lie within the Little Wittenham Nature Reserve. The director, Dr Stephen Head, started out as an ecologist studying coral reefs in the Red Sea; and his office is full of finds gathered in from around the world. He shows me a mammoth tooth found by the river at Wittenham and a fossilized piece of wood still visibly riddled with teredo worms. Most but not all of the coral comes from the Red Sea. Indeed, Dr Head informs me that there is a coral reef on the Thames, at Wytham Great Wood, one of Oxford University's more natural amenities, and 'probably the most studied wood in England'.

Owned by the Northmoor Trust, Little Wittenham Nature Reserve is itself a child of benign scientific innovation. The trust was set up by Sir Martin and Audrey Wood in the sixties, a time when they were still getting their scientific company, Oxford Instruments, off the ground. To begin with, the trust's resources were limited, but that changed thanks to Oxford Instruments' prodigious success with their development of nuclear magnetic resonance scanning. By the early eighties, the trust was in a position to buy the clumps, and to outbid the shooting syndicate that was also interested in purchasing Wittenham Wood.

The Woods, who now live in the manor at Little Wittenham, remain patrons of the trust, which owns 300 hectares, and employs a full-time staff of over twenty in a considerable programme of activities. Conservation may have been at war with science and industrial progress for people such as William Morris, Paul Nash and Robert Gibbings, the wood-engraver and author of *Sweet Thames Run Softly* who lived at Little Wittenham in the fifties, but a different ethos prevails nowadays.

Little Wittenham is certainly not the kind of reserve in which an exhausted 'nature' is merely left alone to rest. It is devoted to projects in which conservation and scientific method walk hand in hand. The trust's farming policy is intended to strike a new and active balance between agriculture and wildlife: it proceeds on the assumption of 'a strong scientific base' and is decidedly not organic. Researchers at the trust's centre for genetic tree improvement at Paradise Farm are seeking to establish that the common walnut tree, *Juglans regia*, has more capacity for improvement as a timber-producing tree than the black walnut, *Juglans nigra*, favoured by European researchers. A new backwater is being cut into the Thames, one of several innovations designed to encourage the rare population of Great Crested Newts in Wittenham Wood. The Great Dodder, a rare parasitic plant, tried to vanish from the riverside at Wittenham shortly after the banks were closed to anglers, but it wasn't allowed to depart so easily. A briskly launched research programme revealed that the anglers had had the unexpected virtue of exposing Dodder seed to light as they churned up the soil along the silted bank. So a carefully managed amount of seasonal tramping will be encouraged from now on.

This active approach to conservation does not automatically find itself in harmony with more aesthetic ideas of the spirit of place: a fact that became evident when the trust started to implement its plan for the trees in Wittenham's much-loved clumps. By the early eighties, the hill-top beeches that Paul Nash had painted were around 250 years old. Some had fallen but others were dying back and even teetering. The trust's forestry consultant pointed out that the clumps were dangerous and that the public were moving about freely in them. Reluctant to fell the trees in one swoop, the trust diverted a public footpath through the Round Hill clump, fenced it off, and started a replanting programme which increased the wooded area on top of both hills.

This was done in consultation with concerned local authorities and the public, but it was still a delicate negotiation, which revealed potential fault lines between beauty and silvicultural practice. Trees are not eternal, especially when they are beeches planted in exposed positions, and yet, for some people in the area, Wittenham Clumps were also symbols of a timeless Englishness of

Paul Nash's kind, and any extension or change in them seemed like a kind of desecration.

Certainly, there can be no replacement for the 'Poem Tree' – an aged beech which stands on the top of Castle Hill, dead and rotting, its branches sawn off for safety reasons, but the trunk retained on account of the now illegible poem inscribed in its bark. The perpetrator of this wooden anthem was one Joseph Tubb, who lived not far away in Warborough Green and had been in the habit of walking up to the clumps, where he carved his tribute in 1844. A paean of praise to the ancientness of the clumps and their surrounding landscape, his poem conjures up ruthless Danes, Mercians and powerful Romans, all of whom were once to be found 'yonder there where Thames smooth waters glide'. A work of limited literary distinction, the poem on the Poem Tree nevertheless remains superior to the expostulations carved by more recent visitors.

The Poem Tree also remains a shrine of remembrance to this day – and not just to the anonymous person or people who come and plant hyacinths and other garden centre bulbs in its rotting roots. When I visited it one Sunday morning after the vernal equinox in March, I found a party of young Druids encamped in a hollow just next to it. They had evidently been there overnight, capering through the storm in white sheets that now hung drying in the branches nearby. They had dressed the clump with floral wreaths, and drawn pagan swirls on the turf around a chosen tree with wholemeal flour.

CULHAM: New Uses for Thames Water

For Joseph Tubb, the view from Castle Hill prompted a meditation on the inevitable 'course of time' and 'the wreck which fate / and awful doom award the earthly great'. That hard fact remains, but to look out from the clumps nowadays is to see something quite other than the evocative ancientry of the 1840s. The triumph of the machine could hardly be writ larger anywhere. The pub in Long Wittenham may be called 'The Machine Man', but Didcot power-station represents mechanism on a quite different scale. A vast coal- and oil-fired facility with enormous cooling towers, it dominates the entire area – reducing the

Dyke Hills of prehistoric Dorchester to mere wrinkles in the meadow, over-whelming the White Horse at Uffington, and making molehills of the clumps themselves. Didcot power station may find no place on the current map of the Thames and its river path, but it looms as satanically as a monstrous mill can do. It also sucks large quantities of water out of the Thames, using it for cooling purposes and then discharging it back into the river.

Another relic of the postwar military-industrial complex stands on the downs some five miles south of Abingdon. Originally the RAF base from which troop-bearing gliders set off for Arnhem in the Second World War, Harwell was taken over by the Atomic Energy Research Establishment in 1946 and built up into a vast nuclear complex headed by Sir John Cockroft. For years, Thames water was used to cool Harwell's atomic reactors, too – pumped out of the river at Sutton Courtenay and returned at Culham. In the early decades, Harwell was shrouded in secrecy – a large and isolated complex, ominous even if it never did exactly glow by night, and connected, in reality as well as public apprehension, with the nuclear weapons programme at Aldermaston and also the nuclear power programme which came into its own at Windscale. The reactors have since been shut down and decommissioned.

The airfield at Culham, much closer to Wittenham Clumps, used to be the base of the Fleet Air Arm, but it was acquired by the Atomic Energy Authority in 1960, and put to use as an open rather than secret site. Like Harwell, it is now a science park, with a high-tech atmosphere and public sculptures made of neatly engineered concrete. Many of its buildings are occupied by a company called AEA Technology, which was hived off from the state-owned UKAEA in September 1996, in the last privatization of the Conservative era, and which has since demonstrated that the science and technology of nuclear research can find profitable application in new fields.

AEA Technology certainly has its share of defence and space-related contracts, but it has also been taking a high-tech approach to the deciduous leaf – seen here not as a motif on a piece of Kelmscott chintz but as a problematic object that may cause trains to skid on a Thames valley railway line. A device being designed for Thames Trains will register that the train's wheels are skidding, and then signal to the control room via a global positioning satellite, thus making it possible to pinpoint exactly where the blockage lies.

Some 880 of AEA Technology's post-nuclear staff are committed to recon-necting technology and the environment in a profitable way. As I walked through the place I heard strings of clever and animated people insisting that their science was now at the service of the environment, and not its possible destroyer. Remembering the toxic and clouded swamp that Richard Jefferies made of London in his novel *After London*, it seemed that there was hardly an element of that late nineteenth-century nightmare that these scientists aren't getting sorted out. They help governments and private companies with energy efficiency and reducing emissions, have an oil-spill team, run the National Chemical Emergency Centre, specialize in the 'remediation' of contaminated brown field sites, and are developing new ways of 'washing' polluted soil and also of 'bio-remediation' in which bacteria are used to eat up pollutants. Even the willow tree, so well loved by William Morris, has been enlisted in this endeavour: an excellent device, I was assured, for sucking heavy metals from contaminated ground.

AEA Technology's experts in Computational Fluid Dynamics may originally have used their computer simulations to predict flows in nuclear reactors, but they now work on a contractual basis, modelling the movement of liquids or gases through all sorts of systems for clients all over the world. These software engineers have modelled the movement of blood in arteries and of air in domestic products such as vacuum cleaners and hover lawn-mowers. They've modelled the fire at King's Cross station, the ventilation system to be used in the Millennium Dome, and even the progress of tidal surges up the Thames estuary. 'The Thames has always challenged our software,' says a spokeswoman, helpfully.

It was among the staff of the unprivatized organization UKAEA that I encountered yet another man called William Morris. A scientist rather than a socialist visionary or a philanthropic motor magnate, William Morris III is responsible for research in a project designed to find benign civil uses for a ther-monuclear process that found its first incarnation in the hydrogen bomb. The 'fusion' project is seeking to replicate the process occurring in the core of the sun. Its raw materials are two different forms of hydrogen: deuterium, which is

Abingdon. The MG factory has closed, but tradition still obliges local dignitaries to throw buns at the populace on special occasions.

found in water, and tritium, which is manufactured using lithium.

The UKAEA's fusion scientists explain that these fuels, water and lithium, are readily available. Unlike fission, fusion produces no atmospheric pollution and leaves no radioactive waste materials to be processed or removed. It is, they say, the safe, sustainable, environmentally-friendly form of nuclear power.

Originally a secret project, pursued in connection with the Atomic Weapons Research Establishment at Aldermaston, the search for a controlled fusion process was well underway by the mid-fifties, a time when over-confident scientists predicted that huge areas – say the entire east coast of America – would be powered by cheap, perhaps even free, fusion-produced electricity in fifteen years' time. Fired partly by the arms race of those years, a fusion machine called ZETA ('Zero Energy Thermonuclear Assembly') was the first to be built in this experimental stretch of the Thames valley.

ZETA became Britain's answer to Russia's Sputnik spy satellite, and senior Harwell scientists were soon being quoted in the US press, insisting that Britain was ahead of the Americans, when it came to 'harnessing the power of the Hydrogen bomb for peaceful purposes'.

Since then, the fusion project has been transferred to Culham Science and

Engineering Centre, and ZETA, which was less successful than claimed at the time, has fallen back into prehistory. The current range of experimental reactors are called Tokamaks, after the first such apparatus in which Soviet scientists used powerful magnetic coils to keep the hydrogen plasma away from the walls of its containing vessel, thus making greater heat possible and opening the way to considerable Soviet breakthroughs in 1969.

Having looked at UKAEA's spherical Tokamaks, I wondered how long it might be before controlled thermo-nuclear fusion ever becomes an economic source of power. The question remains open. William Morris III remarks that the basic physics of magnetically contained fusion is largely understood. The challenge is to generate more energy by fusion than is required to heat the plasma sufficiently to initiate the process, and in that endeavour the main rule is 'the bigger the Tokamak the better'.

Enter, then, the European Community. A building just around the corner in Culham science park houses JET, or 'Joint European Torus', a much larger Tokamak which has been functioning since 1983. The flagship of the EC's fusion projects, JET has employed an international workforce of approximately 700 in a programme intended to develop 'magnetic confinement fusion' as a 'new clean source of safe and environmentally-friendly energy'.

JET has certainly helped to internationalize this stretch of the Thames: there is a European School, near Culham, and 'boules' is played in some pubs in the White Horse Vale. It has also, so its advocates claim, brought controlled fusion almost to its break-even point, where the amount of energy generated is equal to that taken to create the reaction. The scientists at the JET project have developed a detailed design for an even bigger and better Tokamak that would make it possible to trigger a fusion process with the critical mass to sustain itself for a considerable period, thus generating a vast stream of surplus energy. This proposed International Thermonuclear Experimental Reactor (ITER), could conceivably now be built as the world's first Tokamak power station. But it would cost at least £6 billion, and that sum, as Dr Paul Thomas volunteers, is presently not realistic.

The quest for 'fusion' is quite some project to find sitting on the banks of the Thames; and only time will tell whether the spherical Tokamak will eventually be seen to have been useful, or just another gargantuan twentieth-century folly which absorbed vast sums of money and then came to almost nothing. When I asked Christopher Carpenter of UKAEA how long the fusion process could be kept going just using the hydrogen in the water filling the Thames above Teddington Lock, he confidently anticipated that it might be enough to outlast the human species. He surprised me even more when he declared William Morris, the one at Kelmscott rather than just down the corridor at Culham, to be 'one of my great heroes'.

LOCKS: The View from Afar

This internationalized, high-tech stretch of the river is surely strange enough to defy any ordinary Thames guide, and yet there is one 'book of the river' which seems curiously suited to its atmosphere. To find it, we must go back to Little Wittenham, where Sir Martin Wood remembers walking out one day in the early eighties, and meeting a Japanese gentleman who was unusually interested in Day's Lock, just down the lane. The man turned out to be HIH Crown Prince Naruhito, also known as Prince Hiro, the eldest son of Emperor Akihito and Empress Michiko. He was in Oxford for two years from 1983 to 1985, based at Merton College and carrying out research into commodity transportation on the eighteenth-century Thames.

Prince Naruhito's dissertation, 'The Thames as Highway; a Study of Navigation and Traffic on the Upper Thames in the Eighteenth Century', was never exactly published. But a private edition was printed at the Oxford University Press in 1989 – with an appropriately respectful Foreword by the Crown Prince's supervisor, Peter Mathias, who observes, quite rightly, that Naruhito's study does not 'follow in the tradition of sweet Thames run softly'. As a work of economic history, Naruhito's study is quite free of pastoral illusion, and focuses instead on the working river as it was when the Thames basin was 'the greatest hinterland for the supply of agricultural produce to London'. Prince Naruhito may inevitably live at some remove from ordinary life at home, but he got remarkably close to the forgotten bargeowners, haulers and lock-keepers who worked the Thames when it was 'the greatest river system in the south of England': close enough, certainly, to make what his supervisor describes as 'a substantial contribution to our knowledge about river transport in the eighteenth century'.

Prince Hiro presents his findings modestly – styling his book as no more than 'an interim report', which he hoped would make 'some contribution to the research of others who share the same interest with me'. His is a Thames of round-bowed flat-bottomed barges, large and small: vessels which were pulled upriver both by horse and human labour, with or without the assistance of sail. Groundings were frequent, since the river was always inclined to be too dry.

The vessels going downstream may have carried cheese from Lechlade and Abingdon, corn, malt, even paper from near Cookham. But the barges travelling upstream from the Thames and Severn Canal Company's wharf in London brought an extraordinary assortment of goods in the opposite direction – maize, tobacco, tea, liquor and spirits; grease, tallow, pelts and timber; sash windows, garden rollers and also crates of books. Some of the bargemasters, meanwhile, appear to have lived well, despite the many tolls and taxes they would find themselves paying along the length of the river. HIH Prince Naruhito notes that some even had mahogany furniture in their homes.

Two engineering developments assisted this growth in trade on the river. The first was the development of an extensive canal system. The Thames and Severn Canal, which ran from the Severn to the Thames at Lechlade, was opened in 1789. The Oxford Canal came down from Coventry, while the Kennet and Avon Canal joined Bristol to the Thames at Reading in 1810. The Wiltshire and Berkshire Canal was cut into the river at Abingdon in 1809.

Yet Naruhito was also much interested in the machinery of the river, and in particular the weirs and locks. Traditionally, weirs had been built by fishermen and millers, and, to begin with, say from the thirteenth century, the typical lock was a flash-lock – a single opening in the weir which was controlled by paddles which could be raised to release water. Barges would have to 'ride the cascade' downstream and be winched or dragged up through the lock by horses and haulers. These locks were hazardous to navigate and there was an obvious conflict of interest between the bargemasters, who needed to pass through, and the millers who lost their head of water when the lock was opened. Indeed,

THE SOURCE TO GORING: MACHINES IN THE GARDEN

Prince Hiro reveals that large boats were causing problems on the Thames long before the coming of the 'cocktail-bar cruisers' of recent decades. Big barges obliged lock-owners to enclose large amounts of water in order to float these vessels through on a 'high flash' – a process which was likely to cause delays, to irritate millers and fishermen who lost their water in the process, and also to flood agricultural land.

Such were the difficulties that in 1795, the Thames Commissioners ordered that the flash-locks below Reading could only be opened twice a week. By that time, the future was known to lie in a new kind of double- or pound-lock, with two gates and an enclosed chamber, that had been familiar in Holland from the sixteenth century. On the Thames, however, the story begins in the area just downstream from Oxford, thanks to the Oxford–Burcot Commissioners of 1620, who were charged with making the river properly navigable up to Oxford. Due to their endeavours, three pound-locks were installed along this stretch of the Thames in the early seventeenth century: a transformation that eased the shipping of coal and stone from Headington, near Oxford. Two of these new locks were at Iffley and Sandford, both now within the broader area of Oxford. Another was at Swift Ditch, an artificial cut at Culham, which appears to have offered the bargemasters of old a riparian equivalent of an Abingdon bypass. It was thanks to these improvements, as Prince Naruhito duly records, that the first barge reached Oxford from London on 31 August 1635.

From the 1770s onwards, the Commissioners for the River Thames were charged with upgrading the river. Seventeen new pound-locks had been built above Maidenhead by 1791, and a tow path had been created, too, for the use of horses as well as casual labourers known as 'halers'.

These improvements greatly increased the trade on the Thames. Some 600 barges were soon operating above Maidenhead, and HIH Crown Prince Naruhito was able to measure the increase in trade through the case of one essential Thames commodity. 'What is Malt?' he asks with that more scientific than pastoral shine in his eye. 'Malt is the generic name given to barley or other grain prepared for brewing or distilling. Beer, gin and whisky were all made from malt.' Traditional Thames-side stuff, then. But for Naruhito malt was a crucial substance because of the excise duty that was levied on it at the time of its manufacture. This could be reclaimed if excised malt was lost or spoiled in the river; and fortunately for Naruhito's purposes, all such claims had to be proved in the Courts of Quarter Sessions, whose proceedings were duly recorded.

So Naruhito is able to tell us that, in 1749, John Grain's barge sank at Goring, losing 75 quarters of malt; and that, on another occasion, John Soundy of Henley sank near Staines Bridge with 193 quarters in all, which was judged to be totally spoiled having lain under water for several days. The 'sinking of malt' became a scientific tool in the hands of this student: a way of gauging the extent of traffic, the capacity of barges and the reduction in accidents that followed the introduction of pound-locks, which are consequently proved to be benign devices in the book of HIH Crown Prince Naruhito.

The Boating Pavilion in Streatley-on-Thames, by Brookes Stacey Randall, a young architectural practice that is determined not to 'ape' traditional styles.

STREATLEY AND GORING:
A New Building in an Old Gap

We leave this stretch of high-tech England a few miles south of Wallingford at the Goring Gap, where the Thames cuts through the chalk ridge that extends across England from the Dorset coast to the Wash. Accumulated over twenty-five million years, this ridge has been described as the 'greatest challenge' in the course of the Thames.[20] It has been suggested that the river might have worked its way through a fissure or fault in the chalk, or that, as the Ice Age receded, a huge lake formed here, like the one that Richard Jefferies imagined pouring through the 'Straits of White Horse' in *After London*, and then brimmed over, scouring away the chalk, rather as the sea went over the sea-wall at Canvey Island in January 1953.

This glacially-assisted break opened a route for invasion and commerce from the coast into the heart of England and, as Thames valley Eurosceptics may be horrified to hear, it also ensured that, in prehistoric times, the Thames was merely a tributary of the Rhine. According to J.R.L. Anderson, 'the final break with the Rhine, as England's final break with Continental Europe, is relatively recent,' which is to say that it occurred at around 6000 BC.

In our less geological timescale, the Thames has been content to divide the villages of Goring and Streatley as it meanders through the Goring Gap. Walk downstream from the bridge on the Goring side and you'll find the area's most enigmatic novelty standing on the opposite bank in a cluster of oak and ash trees, at the bottom of a lawned four-acre garden belonging to a large but architec-turally undistinguished bungalow.

A rectangular box made of glass with a green metal frame, this latest addition to the river bank is cantilevered up over the Thames by two wooden legs joined to its copper base. Streatley's 'Boating Pavilion' is an unashamedly contemporary building, which betrays not the slightest touch of mock Edwardianism or red-brick pastiche. Neither timber framed nor equipped with the mandatory pitched roof, it was designed by the architectural practice Brookes Stacey Randall for an elderly client who wanted a place from which to view the river and entertain guests at any season he might choose.

I asked Nik Randall, who showed me around this curious addition to Thames architecture, if his practice had been consciously striking out against what William Morris called the 'Cockneyfication' of the river. He observed that it would be hard to think of anywhere that was 'more Miss Marples' than Streatley and Goring, adding that 'a lot of people in Britain still aspire to the values of the lower aristocracy. Whether it is a matter of buildings or of dress, they buy in without thinking.' The Boating Pavilion represents a little blow against this 'aping culture'.

'We call it our South Bank project,' says Randall, a cheeky reference to the grandiose glass canopy that Sir Richard Rogers once imagined stretching over the Hayward Gallery and Queen Elizabeth Hall at the South Bank Centre in

London. Designed to harmonize nature and modern technology, it suggests a world in which the age-old battle between the machine and the garden has at last been overcome.

The Streatley Boating Pavilion is the work of an architectural practice which is content, in Randall's words, to think of 'people's lives being slightly improved by what we've done'. It is a minor but pleasant edifice: a teasing and inde-terminate work by architects who don't really mind if we can't work out whether they have added a building or a work of public art to the Thames. Unfortunately, this confusion has already proved too much for one fellow, who has taken a pot-shot at the Streatley Boating Pavilion from the Goring side of the river and put a nasty chip in the middle of the one transparent wall which is made of laminated rather than toughened glass.

VIKINGS IN RICHMOND

Richmond Bridge Boat-houses may hire out yellow bicycles along with its wooden boats, but the man at the centre of this company's operations, Mark Edwards, does his best to remain a traditional Thames boat-builder. He works from a cavernous warren of workshops and boat-houses which starts under Richmond Bridge and extends, in fits and starts, through the drunken horde that, on a fair summer's evening, may cover the entire length of Quinlan Terry's classical river-front development. An ornate barge, owned by Jesus College Oxford, is moored at his pontoon, waiting for some enterprising chancer to reopen it as a floating restaurant, but Edwards's own boats are less pretentious punts, dinghies and skiffs, both single and double.

He remarks that, while traditional wooden boats like his may indeed have seemed doomed in the fifties and sixties, things were already picking up a little by 1980, when he restarted renting out hooped and covered camping skiffs of the sort featured in Jerome K. Jerome's 1889 story *Three Men in a Boat*. There was a time when Edwards had to resort to motorboats, but he gave them up a few years ago. Aware of four or five other traditional boat-yards further up the Thames, he reckons now to be the only one that concentrates entirely on what he calls 'unpowered boats'.

He's got a six-oared cutter, just built on the order of the Tallow Chandlers for use at a rowing club near Putney. Elsewhere, in an oozing cavern directly beneath one of Quinlan Terry's upmarket bars, he shows me a canoe – a beautiful Canadian-style built of cigar-box cedar in the 1880s by Burgoyne's of Hampton Wick. Its owner was Dr Down, a physician whose name is more generally remembered for its association with Down's syndrome rather than the more or less Red Indian canoe in which he used to paddle his comfortably disposed wife.

The most impressive of all Mr Edwards's wooden boats, however, is a wherry,

Previous pages
Edwardian heyday. The Thames at Henley during regatta week, 1908.

a large oar-powered vessel that looks paradoxically ancient but also brand new. Further down the tidal zone, a variety of Thames barges and fishing smacks have been preserved, but there is not one original Thames wherry left. So, when Edwards decided to build his own, he had to copy the design from an old apprentices' model of 1781, which he found in the Science Museum.

Besides making and repairing traditional Thames boats, Edwards has a theory about their history. Standing by his wherry, he insists that, like the traditional Thames skiff, it is really 'a very direct ancestor' of the Viking longships which brought such havoc to the Thames in the ninth century. The wherry has oars and two pointed ends, like a longship, and its hull is not just clinker-built, but made of only five broad planks. The Viking longboat might have run to six, but certainly not the ten or twelve much narrower planks normal for even the smallest of coastal boats. The ships of the raiding Norsemen were made of very rigid construction, which was well suited to river use, and, as Edwards remarks, it was on the Thames, above all, that the legacy lived on. Anywhere else, that would be called the gunnel, he says, whacking the thick board forming the top edge of his wherry's hull. 'But here on the Thames, it's called the sax board,' which is surely no coincidence since 'it is where the Vikings hung their sea axes'.

The methods and designs used by coastal boat-builders went through considerable change over the centuries, but on the Thames skills were passed down more or less unmodified from father to son, and their methods remained quite primitive. Indeed, once they had adopted Viking techniques, the Thames boat-builders seem to have stuck with them right into the nineteenth century. Boat-builders elsewhere may had learned to use a process called 'lofting', in which a line drawing is converted into a three-dimensional shape. 'But we don't do anything like that,' says Edwards. 'We don't start with drawings.'

It's a particular art, that of the traditional Thames boat-builder, and its practitioners have long had to balance the threat of redundancy with the canny exploitation of other opportunities. In the 1930s and 1940s, some of the river's craftsmen applied their skills in three-dimensional shape construction to the manufacture of aircraft. More recently, one of them, a boat-builder called Jim Smith, who used to work at Thorneycrofts' boat-yard on Platts Eyot near Hampton, even brought his Viking skills to bear on the construction of Concorde's nose.

LEISURE – USES AND ABUSES

Yet, if there are ancient continuities here, Thames boat-building has certainly not been immune to change. Indeed this traditional craft experienced its biggest boom in the nineteenth century following the watery revolution which inaugurated what the historian Patricia Burstall has described as 'The Golden Age of the Thames'.[1]

It was partly due to the railways that the non-tidal Thames, which had passed its peak as a working waterway linked to canals, was reborn in the 1870s as 'the chief pleasure resort of Southern England'. Central to this change was an extraordinary transformation in the social status of rowing itself. Once conceived as mere labour best left to rough-tongued and horny-handed watermen, rowing became a desirable activity among the upper classes. The watermen of London had long competed for cash prizes in their own annual 'Doggett's Coat and Badge Race', but no mere 'race' was good enough for the new upriver 'amateurs'. They preferred the Venetian word 'regatta', which soon became part of the language of the Thames. New regattas were started up at Cookham, Windsor and Eton, Marlow and, of course, Henley; and with them came a seasonal riot of Venetian fêtes, waterside concerts, *tableaux vivants*, Chinese lantern and fireworks displays. The river on which bargees had once struggled to get through weirs now sported exotic new attractions: Venetian gondoliers, blacked-up entertainers who made their money by 'niggering' from less elegant boats, and distinguished foreign visitors like the King of Siam, who stayed at Taplow Court in 1897.

Towns like Maidenhead thrived on this transformation: its riverside hotel Skindles becoming a famous destination, much cited in the divorce courts, where guests could expect to be entertained, or perhaps just irritated, by performers from the river – including, on one occasion, a couple who managed to sing a Verdi duet to the accompaniment of a piano anchored at midstream on a punt.

The rise of leisure even changed the pollutants floating down the river. Along with slops from the houseboats and the odd dead dog and even suicide, as reported by Jerome K. Jerome, visitors could now expect to find large numbers of corks and empty champagne bottles eddying just downstream from every town. Lord Desborough recorded another kind of refined debris, objecting that there were places where strawberries and lettuce leaves had combined in sufficient quantities to form a 'messy mass' on the surface of the river.

The boat-builders rode this new wave, too, shifting upstream from places like Lambeth or Wandsworth, and resettling in Putney, Richmond, Eton, Maidenhead, Henley and Oxford – it seems that almost every place on the upper Thames that got a railway station, had a boat-yard shortly afterwards. Already transmogrified into a wherry and skiff, the Viking longship now mutated into a continuously improving racing boat with lowered sides, outriggers, swivel rowlocks and eventually also sliding seats. There was a great market for leisure boats, too: no wherries any longer, but whole fleets of punts, rowing gigs, funnies, skiffs, whiffs and randans, the latter being an odd vessel in which a sculler with two oars would sit between two single oars. For that brief period in the 1880s, there were also Canadian canoes like the one that belonged to Dr Down.

If the years between 1870 and 1914 represented the Golden Age of the Thames, they also saw the upper river become a place where class antagonism found new forms of expression, unbridled by the conventional disciplines of the settled community or workplace. The regattas, fêtes and races (whether of boats at Henley or horses at Ascot) forming the main events of the season may have been of an upper-class disposition, but the river of leisure also had to accommodate legions of working-class excursionists, generically known as 'Arry and 'Arriet in the toffee-nosed reportage of the time. Riparian landowners found themselves at war with campers who, if the landowners' complaints are to be believed, chopped up their trees for firewood, to say nothing of their shrubs and even their voluntarily placed litter-boxes. Mild-mannered and discerning bird-watchers found themselves lined up against fleets of gun-toting desperadoes bent on the assassination of kingfishers. Once quiet backwaters were said to be

Boulter's Lock, Maidenhead: once notorious as a site of class warfare between drunken onlookers and leisurely gentlefolk travelling on the river.

crammed with punts full of drunkenness and amorous misdemeanour. There was foul language on the streets of genteel towns, and concentrated aggravation at places like Boulter's Lock in Maidenhead, where drunken 'lock-loungers' apparently thought nothing of tossing grape-skins into the laps of genteel ladies in passing punts, and then laughing into the spluttering faces of their husbands.

The emergence of the Thames as a place of leisure affected other venerable river customs, including the greeting that was traditionally exchanged between passing boats. In an article printed in *The Spectator*, 20 May 1712, Joseph Addison describes travelling on the London Thames with his fictional, old-fashioned friend Sir Roger de Coverley. Embarking for a pleasure garden one evening at Temple Stairs, they were rowed by a waterman with a wooden leg. Sir Roger was moved to hear that this fellow had lost the original while fighting the French, and he launched into a patriotic expostulation, commending the Thames as 'the noblest river in Europe' and hailing London Bridge as 'a greater Piece of Work than any of the Seven Wonders of the World'.

Being of genial as well as patriotic disposition, Sir Roger de Coverley also had the habit of greeting all passing boats with a polite salutation. On this occasion, however, he was greatly surprised to hear his 'Good-night' returned in the rudest form by a young fellow who 'asked us what Queer old Putt we had in the Boat; and whether he was not ashamed to go Wenching at his Years'. Sir Roger de Coverley may have been outraged by this example of 'Thames ribaldry', but he had actually fallen victim to a well-established custom, according to which people sailing on the Thames would 'accost each other in the most abusive language they could invent' and with 'as much satirical humour as they were capable of producing'.[2] It is said that in one of these fluvial contests, Dr Samuel Johnson triumphed with the retaliatory remark: 'Sir, your wife, under pretence of keeping a bawdy house, is a receiver of stolen goods.' A virtuoso stroke, which may well have reduced the opposition to puzzled silence.

By the late nineteenth century, the Thames insult had moved upriver, but it remained undiminished as an act of class warfare. Many such exchanges must have passed between the upright Etonian sculler and the lower-class excursionist; and we know from Jerome K. Jerome's *Three Men in a Boat* that words both hot and sly also flew between punting skiffs and steam launches taking pompous toffs and aristos upriver for the Henley Regatta. Jerome describes how he and his fellows conducted their own hostilities against these 'bumptious' vessels, convinced that 'the expression on the face of the man who, with his hands in his pockets, stands by the stern, smoking a cigar, is sufficient to excuse a breach of the peace by itself; and the lordly whistle for you to get out of the way would, I am confident, ensure a verdict of "justifiable homicide" from any jury of river-men'. Not content with drifting around, as if aimlessly, in mid-stream whenever one of these 'mechanical monstrosities' was sighted, Jerome and his friends enjoyed irritating their lofty passengers by pretending to mistake them for a company of workers out for a beanfeast, asking them 'if they were Messr's Cubit's lot or the Bermondsey Good Templars, and could they lend us a saucepan'.

If rudeness was redefined during the Golden Age of the Thames, so, too, was the English art of vandalism. Churches and abbeys on the river may bear scars left by the iconoclastic seventeenth-century Puritans who broke stained-glass windows and knocked noses off recumbent knights of stone. But at Wargrave, the destroyers came a few months before the First World War, and the fact that they were never apprehended is thought to be a direct consequence of the popularity of the river, which made it impossible to tell one summer visitor from the next.

It was early in the morning on 1 June 1914 that locals heard a crackling noise in St Mary's Church, and discovered it was on fire. The fire brigades were called from Henley, and other nearby towns, but nothing could be done to stem this Whitsun blaze, and, as The Times reported on 2 June, 'one of the most picturesque churches on the banks of the Thames was completely destroyed'. The damage to this 'signally beautiful' church – in the words of the Diocesan Architect 'as nearly complete as it was possible for the evil ingenuity of wickedly disposed people to make it' – was only slightly overstated. The great timbers of the roof were lost, along with the Jacobean pulpit and various seventeenth-century details, but the tower remains standing to this day, the pride of a building that was rebuilt and then reconsecrated in 1916.

Wargrave church was fired by militant Suffragettes who, here as elsewhere, left unmistakable signs of their presence: a hammer, with which they had gained

entry, and three postcards addressed 'To the Government Hirelings and Women Torturers'. They called on the Church of England to 'follow its own precepts before it is too late', and insisted that 'Blessed are those that suffered persecution for justice sake, for theirs is the Kingdom of Heaven'.

The fire at Wargrave was part of a wider campaign of arson and vandalism – *The Times* called it 'a guerilla war upon society' – launched by members of Mrs Pankhurst's Women's Social and Political Union in 1913. Striking back against a government that was force-feeding and otherwise abusing hunger-striking Suffragette prisoners in Holloway and elsewhere, these 'Suffragette criminals' (or 'mad women' as less restrained papers called them) defaced paintings in the National Gallery and burned buildings, including the Prime Minister Lloyd George's new house. Prison doctors were attacked with dog whips, and a bomb was placed under the Coronation Chair at Westminster. Churches seem to have been targeted for their association with the infamous and, as Christabel Pankhurst believed, positively life-threatening contract known as Marriage.

No one was ever charged with setting fire to the church in Wargrave, but speculation has continued to this day. In the mid-sixties, one man recalled how one of the claimed six Suffragettes created a diversion by setting fire to letters in a pillar box and then standing there with a placard reading 'Votes for Women'.[3] According to the same witness, the six women who had fired the church were first handcuffed together around a lamp post, and later made to lie on historically significant gravestones to protect them from fire-damage or from being trampled in the rush to put out the fire.

But this is all make-believe, for no suspects were apprehended. It is said that three likely Suffragettes were seen, masquerading as ordinary summer visitors, near the church on the evening of the fire. There is also talk of two women on motorbikes, an unusual sight at the time. But the culprits escaped capture, despite the best efforts of the two Wargrave ladies who took the train up to Scotland Yard to help identify the offenders from photographs. The most likely conclusion, so I am informed, is that the arsonists had come by train and got off at the wrong station, having intended to go to Shiplake, then the home of a judge who had passed down particularly harsh sentences on other militant Suffragettes.

Opposite **St Mary's Church, Wargrave, after militant Suffragettes visited in June 1914.**

HENLEY ROYAL REGATTA

More than a century later, the country is divided between those who love the Henley Royal Regatta, and those who groan at the very thought of it. I have always belonged in the second camp, which I consequently believe to be much larger than the first. Indeed, I still pin my hopes for England's future on that conjecture.

Henley Royal Regatta may be a particular and thoroughly class-bound event but it has been elevated, with the help of many visiting artists, into a defining image of English life. So it was for the American-born John Singer Sargent, who must himself have been one of the sights of Henley during the summer of 1887. Having rigged up a punt as a floating studio, he could be seen manoeuvring himself around the river wearing white flannel shirt and trousers, with a silk scarf tied around his waist and a ribboned straw boater on his head. Thus attired, Sargent painted 'Two Women Asleep in a Punt under the Willows' and other pleasing, summery studies of ease and leisure.

The traditions of Henley Royal Regatta were still going strong in the early 1930s, when the French painter Raoul Dufy visited. His Henley is a place of parasols, feathered oars, and feathery brush strokes, too. It is a light and fluffy world of bright colours and heraldic flags, all bundled up into what one critic has called 'an explosion of joy and happiness'. Although much admired by some private collectors, these paintings were not well suited to post-war taste. By then, Dufy was seen as 'a virtuoso decorator', who enjoyed playing with the luxurious lights of class privilege. Dufy only confirmed his critics' suspicions when he innocently remarked that 'My eyes are made to efface what is ugly.' Instinctive or not, such a visual manoeuvre seemed irresponsible in an age that was more inclined to view the world as a kitchen sink than as an enchanted regatta full of muscular public school boys. Dufy's stock fell; indeed, his name became synonymous with a tawdry kind of hotel décor. That dismissal may now seem over-harsh, but there is no denying that this visiting French painter does seem to have effaced a good deal more than ugliness from the 'England' of his imagination. As he once wrote to his dealer: 'I have painted the regattas at

Henley, I still have to see the regattas at Cowes and the races at Goodwood, and after that I think that England will be covered!'[4]

So it was with some apprehension that I visited Henley for the closing day of the 1998 Regatta, and some relief that I found the occasion surprisingly tolerable: full of traditional showiness, but also far looser and more relaxed than I remembered from many years before. Indeed, it was like an ancient English totem that had been gently vandalized. The free samples of raspberry sorbet were new, but I recognized the tents and the old boys and the decorative, Dufy-like ladies holding on to their hats and billowing around the Stewards' Enclosure. The family parties having picnics in the car-park were plainly in line with tradition despite their employment of plastic garden furniture, cool-boxes and self-help in place of wicker hampers and butlers. For this opening week of July, Henley is still given over to blazers and boaters, young members of Her Majesty's armed forces, and complimentary copies of the *Daily Telegraph*. But the old protocol of the muscular amateur, raised according to Spartan public-school values, is loosening in a big way. The most genial bunch I met was a crew of Australian oarsmen, returning from a 'Hooray Henry' hunt that had plainly led them through many bars and beer tents. Considerably the worse for drink, but entirely amiable, they were not inclined to apologize for the posthumous state of their maroon blazers, which were darned, patched and held together with staples and safety pins, and generally as gone at the seams as the British Empire. Fine things to drag into the Stewards' Enclosure on the last balmy day of the Regatta.

'Gentlemen will wear lounge suits, jackets or blazers with flannels and a tie or cravat.' Ladies must wear 'dresses or suits with a hemline below the knee'. They should also understand that 'Divided skirts, culottes or trousers of any kind are forbidden.' Perhaps during 'The Golden Age of the Thames' the famous dress code governing the Stewards' Enclosure was merely a description of what upper-class English people would automatically wear to such an event. But the custodians of the dress code now feel obliged to spell out the fact that 'no one will be admitted wearing shorts or jeans'.

As for policing the protocol, that job no longer goes to boater-wearing 'scouts' from Oxford colleges, for whom Henley week once served as a kind of paid holiday. They were judged just a little too rickety and 'amateur' to guarantee Henley Royal Regatta's standards and safety in a world that it has had to share with the IRA, the threat of Libyan terrorists and also Class War, the anarchist group which mounted a 'Bash the Rich' assault on the regatta in 1985, and, as Ian Bone of Class War remembers, managed to kick a good number of picnic hampers into the river. Nowadays, the job of securing the regatta goes to younger people, some of them recruited from the military academies.

The racing lanes are known as Berks and Bucks respectively, and the open water beyond them was plied by a funny fake Mississippi paddle-steamer and various gleaming cocktail-bar cruisers with names like 'My Way'. Loaded with bunting and bottles, these drunken boats chugged up and down the length of Henley

Henley Royal Regatta today, a 'pleasantly aimless affair' with hardly a parasol to be seen.

Reach, some of them stocked with trad-jazz bands playing their own lazy tributes to New Orleans.

Henley must be a bit of a sweat for the competitors, but for the visitors who come here, it is a relaxed and pleasantly aimless affair. Occasionally, a few eights or sculls or fours pass through the jamboree – prompting some of the celebrants briefly to look up from their cups, although not those in the corporate hospitality tents, who sit with their backs to the river watching Wimbledon on TV. This apparent indifference to the races is surely one of the more truly distinctive qualities of Henley Royal Regatta: there can be few athletic events where most people have gone home before the last day on which the finals are held.

Inaugurated in 1839 as a regatta for 'gentleman amateurs', the event became Henley Royal Regatta in 1851, when Prince Albert became its first Royal Patron. Greatly adjusted since then, its significant dates are not just about Cups and Trophy records, but about steps taken, sometimes reluctantly, to open this

Raoul Dufy, 'Regatta at Henley', 1934–52.

formerly exclusive event to the wider world. Henley is a typical English institution, set up on an exclusive set of assumptions, and then opened to the wider public at the slowest rate that is reconcilable with buying off revolution and attack. The definition 'gentlemanly' is no longer used to exclude oarsmen of the 'artisan' class, and the internationalization of Henley's races has greatly increased since 1892, when a Dutchman carried off the trophy for the Diamond sculls.

Women coxes were not allowed until 1975, late by the standards of other regattas; and in a famous incident of 1978 two women scullers, Astrid Ayling and Pauline Hart, put themselves down for the men's double sculls using initials and their maiden names. But 'A. Hohl and P. Bird' were found out just before the race, and all unpleasantness was avoided. Since then, various open events for women have been introduced.

At the end of 1997, the Stewards even decided to 'delete all reference to the

word amateur from the Rules and to introduce the concept of eligibility'. But
the organizers insist that Henley Royal Regatta is still 'amateur' to all intents and
purposes. There are still no money prizes, and the adjustment was only a matter
of falling in with changing rules governing international rowing. 'We don't make
any changes just for the sake of it,' says Pam Cole, who has herself been
employed by the regatta since 1974. 'If it's worked well in the past, we see no
reason to change it.'

Henley Royal Regatta maintains its own rules and governance, and is proud
to conduct itself without commercial sponsorship or external subsidy. Though
somewhat straightened through excavation of the river bank over the years, its
course remains eccentric by international standards, and unlike any other in the
competitive world. Membership has doubled over the last two decades, and a
fifth day was added in 1986.

Yet I noticed some indications of decline. There was hardly a parasol to be
seen anywhere, and the Stewards' Enclosure is no longer the exotic preserve it
used to be. A few splendid iguanas may still lurk in the shadier corners, but the
traditional upper-class look no longer comes with automatic ease – indeed, it is
now divided between dying anachronism and ludicrous parody, with a few
awkward attempts at artificial resuscitation taking place somewhere in between.
Raoul Dufy would probably have been inclined to regret this degeneration,
rather as Dame Barbara Cartland once lamented the decline of London's Oxford
Street, a commercial thoroughfare which she fondly remembered with legions
of tall, handsome and impeccably dressed young English gentlemen prom-
enading along it – elegant and well-mannered figures who, as she recognized
with a snobbish shudder, had long since been replaced by a horde clad in denim,
shell-suits and trainers.

Perhaps it is safer to measure the changes at Henley with the help of a real
old trout. It was at some time near the turn of the century that this unlucky 7-
pound fish leapt out of the well-stocked water near Henley Bridge during
Regatta Week and landed in a punt. The trout was duly photographed and then
cooked and served up at a nearby hotel.[5] An exceptional event at the time, it is
unimaginable that such an event could happen nowadays. The river may be considerably less polluted than in recent decades, but even if serendipity, or the

Environment Agency, could rustle up a 7-pound trout in the Henley Thames today, the fish would be much exercised in finding a suitably placed boat. It might just be able to stun itself against the sides of a passing cocktail-bar cruiser, but mostly this stretch of the water is empty. Old photographs taken from Henley Bridge during Regatta Week, show the river so packed with punts that the exceptional trout would be the one that jumped and did not land in one.

THERAPY FOR TOADS

The upper Thames belongs to 'amateurs' in its literature as well as its competitive rowing. Perhaps that is why it is so much concerned with small, furry animals.

Take Kenneth Grahame, whose story *The Wind in the Willows* was first published in 1908. The author of this Thames classic, which A. A. Milne of Winnie the Pooh fame described as 'a test of character', once expressed his profound relief at not being a professional writer. As Secretary of the Bank of

One of the more archaic of the Thames' annual rituals, swan-upping traditionally involved cutting distinguishing notches into the beaks of those cygnets belonging to the Vintners' Company and the Dyers' Company. The rest, which are left unmarked, belong to the Crown. The picture shows the opening events of 18 July 1932.

England, he was in no need of cash prizes, and felt that literary celebrity and reputation would only get in his way. Writing in his spare time, he was free to produce just what he wanted, taking his time over the construction of clear, simple sentences, and allowing neither pretentious literary artifice nor refined adult judgement to stand mockingly between him and the beloved little animals that he insisted were superior to people in being honest, straightforward and instinctively true to their nature.

Kenneth Grahame, as a friend later pointed out, was 'the eternal boy, keenly alive to the beauty and wonder of the world around him'.[6] Starting out as stories Grahame told to his son 'Mouse', *The Wind in the Willows* was informed by its author's childhood memories of wandering around the upper Thames. In some of his earlier writings, he speaks as a banker, bound to the office routines of Throgmorton Street but dreaming of upriver weekends in 'animal land'. He even hails the Thames-side 'loafer' as a kind of philosopher who 'stands apart supreme', stretched out on the grass or lingering in the inn, quite disengaged from the muscular endeavours of the blazer-wearing and hamper-carrying Argonauts who set off early in their skiffs, punts and canoes.

The riverside world of Ratty, Mole, Badger and Toad has received many tributes since Grahame's time, some of them less expected than others. In the sixties, Pink Floyd were particularly taken by the episode in which the animals scull across a weir pool to the blossomy island where they glimpse the horns and 'shaggy limbs' of Pan. Indeed, they took the title of that chapter, 'The Piper at the Gates of Dawn', and applied it to their first famously 'psychedelic' LP.

But no tributes are as revealing as the one paid by Mr Robert de Board, whom I arranged to meet at the new Henley River and Rowing Museum. He pulled in with a customized number plate, wearing a black leather jacket and a maroon sweater with Burberry of London emblazoned on it in vast letters. We talked about Perpetual, a Henley financial company that has flourished through the age of PEPs and ISAs. We talked about the late Dusty Springfield, who lived and was recently laid to rest in Henley; and we discussed boats, too, including de Board's own Thames slipper launch.

As for *The Wind in the Willows*, de Board declared that he has always loved this book and re-reads it almost every year. Finding himself with twelve weeks off after an operation a couple of years ago, he had sat down to write a sequel that would bring the story into the present.

Entitled *Counselling for Toads: a Psychological Adventure,*[7] Robert de Board's book opens with Mole visiting Toad, only to find Toad Hall run down and Toad himself in a state of abject depression – 'the saddest Toad he had ever seen'. Once so reckless and conceited, Toad has sunk into morbid and immobilizing thoughts and is probably on the bottle, too. So a new animal is introduced, a Heron who, like all counsellors, keeps a box of paper-tissues handy for clients who find themselves suddenly ambushed by their own emotions. And then Toad learns to disclose his secrets, and to encouter his innermost anxieties as prompted by the mentoring Heron's reflective probes – 'So, how did that make you feel?'

'Talking to Toad'll never cure him. He'll say anything.' That was Rat's judgement as expressed to Badger in the original story, but de Board's Heron knows otherwise. While in therapy, his Toad learns to recognize such conditions as the 'Child Ego State' – the characteristics of which are soon enough enumerated on a flip-chart. Having regained a sense of purpose along with new insight through his counselling experience, Toad eventually resolves to relaunch himself as an upmarket London estate agent and Toad Hall is sold to make a management college.

When I asked de Board how he got interested in counselling, he explained that he had started his working life with the aim of becoming a vicar. He had served as Industrial Chaplain to the Bishop of Wakefield for a time, but then, as he told me, he had joined a management training organization called the Industrial Society, which sent him into the docks in London and Liverpool, where he remembers meeting bosses and trade union barons and, over long and unimaginably luxurious lunches, vainly arguing the case against the continued use of casual labour.

It was after that initiation that he became interested in psychoanalysis and, more specifically, in Transactional Analysis, as it applied to group dynamics in organizations. In 1972, he was employed by the Henley Management College to help develop their Management Effectiveness Programme. Now retired, he nevertheless still works at the college, running, or perhaps the word is 'facilitating', a group dynamics course, which is fully booked four times a year.

I was intrigued to hear this, not least because in the early eighties, I, too, worked for the Industrial Society. Like other 'advisers', I was equipped with a bundle of hand-outs and sent into organizations to run short courses on letter-writing, interviewing skills, teamwork and chairing meetings. One of the handouts, I remembered, showed a group of animals sitting around a table for a meeting. The idea was that each creature represented a type of behaviour common in workplaces. One could usually persuade the group to figure out who in their own organization was the twitchy young gazelle, the stubborn and over-forceful boar, or the snake.

While this deliberation went ahead, I would sit there idly wondering at the ease with which a quasi-psychological management culture was spreading through the country which, not so very long ago, had been known as the land of the stiff upper lip and the bloody-minded trade unionist. Efficiency and effectiveness may be desirable goals, but to be a successful employee, especially in a large organization, seemed increasingly to entail disclosing your innermost anxieties at the drop of your line-manager's hat. This humanistic and psychological approach to management was certainly less brutal than its predecessors, but I wondered if it didn't also have the effect of reducing people to the compliant subjects of vast organizational regimes? The time was surely coming, so I thought, to start running courses of the opposite kind. The guiding principles inscribed on the flip-chart would read 'Stay Cool and Admit Nothing'. There would be advice on techniques for concealing your secret anxieties, buttoning up your feelings, evading all psychological probes and not identifying too strongly with your job. No one would, under any circumstances, be allowed to go belly-up and pretend to be a meek and helpless little animal.

HENLEY MANAGEMENT COLLEGE

You can see from the brochure that Henley Management College thinks of the Thames as an enticing lure. The cover photograph shows a clinker-built wooden boat tied up at the bank, and a large white mansion across the river, reposing splendid among trees and verdant lawns sweeping down to the riverbank. Even without the words that are spread across the image – 'focus', 'innovation', 'leadership,' 'imagine' – it is obvious that the mansion is a rich and gleaming destination, while the boat is the Executive Development Programme, or perhaps just the corporate cheque, that will get you there.

Suspend the allegory, and the house reverts to normality as 'Greenlands', the principal building of the Henley Management College, and one that, in the words of another brochure, 'stands today as a tranquil seat of academic excellence after surviving the ravages of a more brutal age'. Flattened by Parliamentary cannons in the English civil war, rebuilt as an Italianate mansion in the early nineteenth century and then further upgraded as the home of W.H. Smith, Greenlands is now 'a testament to the tenacity of visionaries determined to improve industry through high-quality management training'.

Management is surely the triumphant creed of our times. Many other 'isms' have faded or died, but the business schools and management consultants are making a killing as they go down: churning out buzzwords, replacing politics with public relations, squeezing cost-benefit ratios into places where some would prefer conscience still to reside. Though proud of its place on the Thames, Henley Management College positions itself in the middle of this global marketplace – even listing its telephone number with the international dialling code.

Yet because it was in on the management game early, Henley Management College also claims to be a contrary initiative, an evangelizing project formed against the grain of its times. The founding impulse goes back to the years just after the Great War, when a Rowntree-funded 'Management Research Group' concluded that 'the growth of the democratic spirit in the advanced industrial countries spells disaster for the leader in business who attempts to exercise a purely personal control'. The manager, in other words, could no longer strut around like a tyrant born to power.

Opened by the Labour Prime Minister Clement Attlee in 1948, Henley College was established as a staff college for industry and commerce, which pioneered new learning methods, too. Flip-charts were still several decades away, but Henley was quick to spurn the lecture format as an inefficient method of communication favoured by university dons largely because it enables them to display their own learned status. Instead, the college devoted itself to 'syndicates', or small discussion groups which would enable people from diverse backgrounds to reflect on chosen problems.

Interested to see how much of this contrary perspective survives, I drove out of Henley-on-Thames, and headed downstream. Passing the inevitable Toad of Toad Hall Garden Centre, I found the Henley Management College shortly afterwards – a cattle grid, a curved drive, and then a handshake with Lynn Stone, the Alumni Services Director, who led me into a panelled room, which, as she explained, has been known as the Morris Room, ever since somebody opened a drawer and saw the words 'Morris and Co.' hammered into it. Installed when the house was owned by the W.H. Smith family, this woody chamber has lordly oak bookshelves, a fine fireplace, and a commanding view of the Thames: an unlikely place in which to plot a revolution in corporate affairs.

Henley Management College promotes leadership on the river bank from 'Greenlands', an Italianate mansion which was once the home of W. H. Smith, the bookseller.

Having seen legions of men in blazers at the regatta, I had asked to meet some of the women who teach at Henley College. The first to arrive, Dr Susan Foreman, was the Lead Tutor in Marketing. She reaffirmed the value of self-managed learning, as opposed to the kind of 'content input' that lecturers in other subjects still employ. But when I asked whether she saw management or marketing as a means of breaking through the inertia of the British class system, she remarked, a little suspiciously, that she had never thought of her work in connection to social class at all. Saying that she goes home to Wigan 'for a dose of reality', she admitted to no interest in 'chaps rowing' either, or, for that matter, in *The Wind in the Willows*, a book she was content to have avoided as a child: it was, she thought, 'southern reading'.

Maureen George, director of the modular MBA programme, told me that Henley Management College conducted itself as 'a classless society', even if the same could not be said for the surrounding stretch of southern England. It was devoted to team-work, which meant 'ameliorating social differences' and 'crossing barriers', be they of class, ethnicity, or gender. 'You can't present yourself as an instant panacea shop, but you've still got to help people get out of that box.'

Since Estelle Bowman is one of Henley's experts on team-building, I asked her if she had any use for small furry animals as training aids. She knew about Robert de Board's *Counselling for Toads*, but if any animal comes to Estelle Bowman's mind as she surveys the present state of British organizations, it is the 'Frozen Rabbit'. Having spent years driving their employees into cautious and defensive kinds of behaviour by the threat of down-sizing and 'Change', many organizations are now wondering why they don't get immediate results when they then turn round and tell those same employees that they've got to be innovative and prepared to make mistakes.

The regatta emerged as a point of contrast in all my discussions here. Indeed, the mere mention of it brings a groan from tutors, and also, so I was assured, from delegates attending courses, too. There is little natural sympathy for 'chaps rowing' at the College, and none at all for the anachronistic dress code of the Stewards' Enclosure. I got the impression that the regatta, with its ludicrous 'skirt police', represented everything about England that Henley Management College would be happy to leave behind.

Yet the river has its uses here, too, which is why hikers following the Thames path along the Berks bank will sometimes look across the water and see strange antics going on in Bucks. Maybe they'll see a handful of disconcerted senior managers trying to recover from the shock of having turned up for one of Estelle's courses only to be asked to 'speak about yourself for a while without mentioning your work'. Perhaps they are chief-executives of NHS hospital trusts who have been sent out to gather their thoughts on a 'reflective individual jaunt' by the river, and are instead on their mobile phones down-loading messages or monitoring the progress of the internal market back home. But the really lucky hikers will pass when a practical exercise in team-work is underway – perhaps the rumoured one that is said to have entailed improvising some sort of floating vehicle, capturing a female creature of unspecified but presumably mammalian type, and transporting her across the river.

ETON COLLEGE: Relocating the Regatta

Something unusual is happening at Eton, and it has nothing to do with the tail-coats and bow-ties worn by beaks and boys alike. These are taken for granted as quite normal on this stretch of the river, along with the armed police who hover round the college gates, minding the current batch of pupil princes through the years which, though strange enough from any ordinary perspective, may bring them as close to normality as a prince can ever get.

Eton has its traditional river rituals like the Fourth of June 'Procession of Boats', in which the current batch of young lords dress up as nineteenth-century seamen and row past the assembled audience in old wooden eights named after ships in Nelson's fleet. At the command of their coxes, who are dressed as admirals and captains of the same period, these young gods stand up perilously in their boats, hoisting their oars upward towards the sky and, in a tribute first performed in the presence of George III, shake flowers and in some cases also heavy vegetables from their boaters into the water, while the enraptured parents and dignitaries gathered on the bank wait for them to fall in.

Yet nobody should make the mistake of thinking Eton is only a backward-looking institution. The college is also responsible for an ever-expanding hole in the ground a few miles upriver, just south of the village of Dorney. Eton College's contractors have been digging here since the mid-nineties. It's an enormous site, directly across the Thames from Oakley Court, a turreted hotel much featured in Bray Studio's Hammer horror films. The dredgers have gouged their way through silted channels where the river once ran. They've unearthed a Roman bridge and various Neolithic finds are duly displayed in a nearby barn. The growing hole conveniently fills with water as soon as it is dug.

Henley Royal Regatta may stick to its eccentric English course, but Eton College's new rowing lake will qualify as a Category B1 course as defined by the guidelines of the Fédération International des Sociétés d'Aviron. Its water will be quite still, unaffected by eddies or tides. It will have a 2000-metre straight without obstructive bends or 'eyots' as the little islands in the Thames are called. It will have eight rowing lanes, rather than the two or three allowed by the

Thames. At 3.5 metres, it will be deep enough to avoid the resistance that drags on boats in shallower water; and the 'return channel' will be separated from the main lake by an island, as the regulations require.

Quite something, then, and Mr John Langfield is at the centre of it all. As Eton's director of rowing, he is more than a schoolmaster who spends his afternoons riding along the river bank on a bicycle while bellowing instructions at a rowing crew through a megaphone. Besides coaching the college's competitive crews and looking after its 400 boats, he runs residential rowing courses through the summer vacation and also directs the college's boat-building company, Eton Racing Boats, which builds boats for the college, and also to the individual specification of external customers. I notice that one or two discontinued wooden models are still lying around in the company's boat-houses across the water from Windsor, but Langfield observes that, beautiful as these relics of the late Viking age may be, serious rowers nowadays wouldn't dream of touching them. Tails and collars may last for ever, but racing boats have to keep up with the times. Those in the current Eton Phoenix Range employ 'the technology of the future', as pioneered in Formula One racing-car construction. Light, stiff, and durable, they are made of pre-impregnated fabrics (carbon and kevlar), which are heat-cured in a mould.

The new rowing lake aspires to the future too. As he showed me around, Langfield expressed little doubt that it would be 'the best facility in England'. I was in no position to doubt that, but I still felt obliged to mention the word 'élitism'. I must have mumbled, however, for Langfield immediately started talking about the 'arboretum' that will be created as part of the development, along with a new nature reserve. He assured me that there would also be facilities for angling and canoeing, although I couldn't imagine who would want to indulge in the latter activity here: an experience that would surely be like trying to ride a bicycle up a motorway.

'We want to use it nearly every day of the year,' says Langfield, but it was not just the college's own crews that he had in mind. He reminds me that Eton College is a charity, and that it is, therefore, entirely appropriate that the rowing lake will be of use to others as well. The Oxford and Cambridge squads will be able to practise for their annual boat race here. And that is only the beginning, since Eton's planners have noted that over 50 per cent of the country's rowers are within one hour's drive of this new amenity. Eton's rowing lake is set to change the face of the river: a hole in the ground that, as some apprehensive onlookers note, is perfectly designed to scoop up previously river-based events by the dozen, and perhaps even to sell television rights to one of Mr Murdoch's many sports channels.

This may be fine by many of the competitive rowers, but it has been causing anxiety on regatta committees up and down the river. Henley Royal Regatta will surely be able to see off the competition and stick to its own pre-metrical course. But at Marlow, which counts its annual event as second only to Henley among Thames regattas, the hard decision is already being faced. Marlow Regatta may manage three lanes rather than Henley's two, but its course is still an imperfect and quirky thing, and polls have already revealed that many of the 240 or so competitors would move in a flash to Eton's new eight-lane facility. Since the regatta cannot afford to lose its competitive edge, there is a sense of inevitability in the air, combined with apprehension on behalf of the town, which stands to lose a lot through the relocation, and also some grumbling resentment of the Environment Agency whose regulations and officious attitude are said to make it more and more difficult to maintain the regatta on a river increasingly dominated by lucratively licensed leisure cruisers.

Asked if he, too, doesn't somewhat regret leaving the Thames, John Langfield admits that the river is 'more alive', while the rowing lake will probably feel a little 'clinical'. But he is not inclined to extend his lamentations much beyond that. For a start, he says, Eton College will continue to use the river: if he has 100 boys rowing at a higher level, there are 400 involved in less competitive and more leisurely ways. And anyway, the 'liveliness' of the river can be far from convenient. Floods can render it too dangerous to use. And there are dangers in the very nature of competitive rowing: 'looking one way and going the other', as Langfield describes it, is surely as good a method as any when it comes to accidentally spearing a passing gin-palace.

Meanwhile, the democratic Thames gets busier with motorized leisure-craft, represented by expanding and new marinas at Bray and Windsor. 'It is a perfectly legitimate way of enjoying yourself on the river,' says Langfield, but it has to be

Etonians in the Fourth of June 'Procession of Boats', 1999. These young men will soon stand up in their boat, point their oars at the sky, and somehow manage to shake the flowers from their boaters into the water without falling in.

admitted that these users are not always co-operative when it comes to letting the racing eights through. Riparian altercations do happen, and Eton boys have to be especially careful, because it only takes one of them to be rude once and 'we're in *The Sun*'. *Three Men in a Boat* was all very well in its time, but John Langfield, who must be counted as one of the great sights of the river, pacing energetically around the college boat-houses in his white bow-tie, is not inclined to romanticize the river as a place of jumbled class encounter. 'It just doesn't work any longer.'

RUNNYMEDE:
Muddy Shoes and the Spirit of Democracy

In some minds the idea of 'the birthplace of democracy' may be associated with the city state of ancient Athens. Along the Thames, however, that label is applied to a watery stretch of meadow at Runnymede. It was to this site, in June 1215, that a reluctant King John rode from Windsor Castle to meet twenty-five rebellious barons, and, under the guidance of the Archbishop of Canterbury, Stephen Langton, to place his reluctant seal on the articles that were later written up as the Magna Carta.

The document consists of an introduction followed by some sixty-three distinct clauses. A number of these are directly concerned with rivers – granting liberties of water as well as of land, maintaining public usage of river banks, and freeing both towns and people from the obligation of building bridges. The thirty-third clause even rules that, in the interests of navigation, all fish-weirs were to be cleared from the Thames and Medway and, indeed, all rivers throughout England.

The exact definition of those 'fish weirs' has since been much debated by Thames historians, but it is for its more general measures, rather than its obscure riparian stipulations, that Magna Carta is remembered. It freed the Church and the City of London from the absolute powers of the monarch, and guaranteed merchants free movement in and out of England. It freed the people from the arbitrary exercise of power, insisting that courts should have juries and hear witnesses; and that no one would be made a justice, constable, sheriff or bailiff, who did not 'know the law of the kingdom and mean to observe it well'. Magna Carta stipulated that standard weights and measures would be introduced for commodities such as wine, ale and corn. It also defended the widows and young children of men who died while 'indebted to the Jews'. The twenty-five barons ensured that no widow would be forced to marry, and also that no man would be arrested or imprisoned 'on the appeal of a woman for the death of any person except her husband'.

Remembered as the charter that established freedom under the law, Magna Carta became a rallying cry for those who knew that rights are more often won than freely given. Its memory would be invoked in later enactments, including the Petition of Right (1628) and the Habeas Corpus Act of 1679, and it finds further echoes in Federal and State constitutions in the United States of America. Countless agitators have ensured that the memory of 'The Charter' reverberates through history: the Chartists of the nineteenth century, anti-colonialists, Suffragists, dockers and constitutional reformers of our own time.

As for the actual site where King John met the barons, the last clause of

Magna Carta describes this as 'the meadow which is called Runnymede between Windsor and Staines'. Some part of that is now owned by the National Trust, and maintained as a place of hard-won rights, of 'Freedom Under Law'; and, thanks to a long-standing habit of transporting these political rights into the very bones of the English people, of national identity, too. Drive in, through gates and lodges commissioned from Lutyens in the thirties, and you find yourself on a flat watery flood plain, a mead to be sure, and also a Site of Special Scientific Interest devoted to maintaining an imperilled native flora and fauna.

After surveying this wide open space, I found myself looking around for something more precise to focus on. Runnymede has long been used as a political yardstick, a meadow for measuring up both allies and enemies. But anyone looking for the exact location where Magna Carta was signed will be disappointed. Some may come here in a spirit of reverent certainty, but, in the absence of any precise site, the democracy that is commemorated at Runnymede will strike other visitors as more of a puzzle: an open-ended question rather than a fully accomplished fact.

These celebrated 'Fields of Democracy' began their existence as a conserved modern landscape shortly after the First World War when the financially-straitened government prepared to sell various stretches of land around the country. Some Crown-owned acres at Runnymede were bundled up as 'Lot 8' and prepared for sale in the early 1920s. The developers hovered in the background in their usual way, and a Magna Carta Society was formed to campaign against the sale. The Prime Minister, David Lloyd George, had reputedly claimed that a permanent funfair might be built there, but the Magna Carta Society was opposed to such a Philistine idea.[8]

The endangered land was eventually bought by Lady Fairhaven, an American heiress who wanted to create a memorial to her late husband, Urban Hanlon Broughton, MP. In all, some 180 acres of the fields of Runnymede were assembled through transactions with many different owners and, in 1931, the aggregated estate was transferred to the National Trust.

So, with the promise that this place of 'popular resort' would receive 'proper supervision', the timeless fields of democracy came to be held for the nation, an inalienable monument dedicated to the 'perpetual memory' of a late

Conservative Member of Parliament for Preston. In 1931, the Fairhavens commissioned Sir Edwin Lutyens to produce the pavilions and lodges that command the entrances to the National Trust's preserved estate; but these additions were not welcomed by all. The local Egham council objected to the buildings, which were said to infringe the Enclosure Act; and, during the night before they were ceremoniously opened by the Prince of Wales on 8 July 1932, a band of freeborn English objectors sprayed creosote over the walls and pillars of these symbolic buildings – an assault that could only partly be hidden, even after a last-minute manoeuvring of evergreen shrubs. These nocturnal vigilantes were never apprehended, but they appear to have been motivated by the belief that the meadows now being turned into 'Runnymede' were really governed by more ancient public rights as 'Egham Common'.

The meadows of Runnymede, where King John placed his seal on the articles of Magna Carta.

So the fields of democracy came to be preserved as a 'beauty spot' and bank-holiday destination. Yet it was not just British visitors who came to pay their respects to the National Trust's newly established shrine to democracy. The idea of Runnymede stirred the hearts of visitors from America, where the founding fathers had fought the British for their own democratic independence, urged on by the writings of Thomas Paine. In 1935, it also moved the Australian leader Robert Gordon Menzies, who visited Britain for the Silver Jubilee of George V, and declared himself profoundly moved to stand on the fields of Runnymede and tap into the 'secret springs' of the 'slow English character'.[9]

Since then, the symbolic acres of Runnymede have been augmented by various symbolic monuments dedicated to remembrance and freedom. The more recent of these place their own seal on the Anglo-American alliance as it was during the years of the Cold War. A superior product of the McCarthy era, the American Bar Association memorial stands on a sloping acre next to the National Trust land, which was donated by Egham Urban District Council. A formal monument among oak trees, it was built in 1957 to commend the Magna Carta as the root of 'Freedom Under Law'.

I was more interested by the Kennedy Memorial, standing a short distance along the same slope, which acknowledges Runnymede as the place where 'the ideal of human rights was born with the signing of Magna Carta'. It is approached by means of a wicket gate which opens on to a winding path rising up through a little stretch of native English wood to the memorial beyond. The wood is enchanting and unconfined, in short a typical English hobbit-grove. The winding path that the landscape architect Sir Geoffrey Jellicoe has rising through this wood was intended to take the visitor on an allegorical journey modelled on John Bunyan's *Pilgrim's Progress*.

The notice by the gate suggests that many visitors have missed this subtle point. Indeed, it seems, that some, perhaps especially Americans, have been inclined to see this informal wood as a terrible mess which would benefit from vigorous strimming. It points out that the 'typical English woodland' is 'intentionally unkempt', while the path is deliberately windy. Similarly, the steps are without uniform shape, not because the builders were incompetent, but because the architect wanted them that way. Made of stone cobbles or 'setts', they have been assembled to ensure that each one has its own scale and individuality.

Visitors are invited to consider the individual 'setts' as being like pilgrims working their way up through 'the wildwood of life' to the shrine above. The meaning of the steps themselves is less clear. Known as the 'Steps of Individuality', it has been claimed that they number forty-seven, one for each year of President Kennedy's life. But, by my count, there were forty-nine, a figure that prompted the local historian Richard Williams to suggest that each one might represent an American state.

The monument itself is perched above this unresolved quandary of a path. A seven-ton rectangular block of Portland stone, it is mounted on a rough-hewn catafalque, and inscribed with words that seal the compact between America and this bit of sacred English ground. Carved by the sculptor Alan Collins, it bears a sentence from President Kennedy's inaugural address: 'Let every nation know whether it wishes us well or ill that we shall pay any price, bear any burden, meet any hardship, support any friend or oppose any foe in order to assure the survival and success of Liberty.' There's a promise in there, but also a threat. Indeed, standing in front of that great slab of stone, I could feel the steely certainties of the Cold War crashing down on Sir Geoffrey Jellicoe's organic and deliberately decentralized woodland, and putting their own bracing interpretation on the 'Steps of Individuality' behind.

Yet there is another oddity about the Kennedy Memorial, which is often revealed by the state of the visitors' boots by the time he or she arrives there from the car park. To get to the Kennedy memorial, you have to walk some distance across the National Trust's land which, being on the Thames floodplain, can be very wet and muddy. It is said that American visitors often step out of their coaches at the car park and express amazement when told that, in the absence of a proper path, they are going to have to trudge across a marsh to their goal. Indeed, some visitors are reported to have voiced this objection even at the opening ceremony on 14 May 1965.

This little awkwardness, acknowledged by the words 'access difficult' in the National Trust's book of properties, reflects an embarrassment that goes back to the moment when the British government announced its intention of building a memorial within a few days of Kennedy's assassination on 22 November 1963. The various options were reviewed, and on 25 March 1964, the Prime Minister, Sir Alec Douglas Home, informed the House of Commons that since 'President Kennedy gave a voice to the heritage which is enshrined for us in Runnymede', the appropriate memorial would be 'an acre of Runnymede, laid out simply, with a simple plinth and steps, which should be given in perpetuity to the United States in memory of President Kennedy'.

However, this proposal was not unanimously well received either locally or by the National Trust, which had evidently not been consulted. On 2 April, a former secretary of the Trust, D.M. Matheson, wrote to *The Times*, observing that the recommendation was 'regrettable', and that the Trust would 'be obliged to oppose the scheme by every means at its disposal…'

The main problem was that the land was 'inalienable', and could not be transferred to another owner, even if the Trust wanted to take that route, without a special act of Parliament. So the authorities had to launch a hasty hunt for land adjacent to the National Trust's estate at Runnymede. This produced the site eventually chosen – three acres rather than one, of Crown land which was then let to a local farmer for grazing purposes.

So the memorial went ahead, with the National Trust only granting pedestrian access across the sacred meadows on condition that it involved no 'works' and was only 'a grass path'. Grumbling letters continued to appear in various papers around the country, but the memorial was opened on 14 May 1965 by the Queen, who strode up Jellicoe's highly individual steps from the wicket gate and stood silent before the monument for two minutes. Mrs Kennedy listened together with her two children, Caroline and John, as five-minute tributes were read out by the Queen and Harold Macmillan, who declared with great emotion that 'every family in Britain felt a sense of personal bereavement'. In her message to the British people, Jacqueline Kennedy described how her husband 'returns today to the tradition from which he sprang', and thanked the creators of the memorial for sharing with her 'thoughts that lie too deep for tears'.

Look closely at the memorial stone, thirty-five years later, and you can just see a spidery web of cracks, repaired but still visible, that stretch over the surface. These testify to the fact that this elegantly conceived monument has not escaped aggression. They were caused by a bomb in October 1968, an act of vandalism that was attributed, rightly or wrongly, to the IRA. The work suffered further indignities in July 1974, when it was pulled over with the help of a steel hawser, and daubed with red paint. These difficulties aside, however, the Kennedy Memorial is holding up pretty well.

ISLANDS IN SUN AND RAIN

Magna Carta Island is one of many little islands in the Thames. Some of these 'aits' or 'eyots' have been created by engineers improving the river, but the majority have been made by the river as it has meandered and spread over the ages. Some bear witness to all but forgotten threads of English history, but after Runnymede it is hard not to see others as little emblematic domains on which various faces of modern English democracy are displayed.

Some are council-owned parks, like Ray Mill Island near Boulter's Lock in Maidenhead, or Penton Hook Island near Chertsey, a public park superimposed over a burial ground from the Great Plague of 1665. Others remain exclusive preserves. Lock Island, near Marlow, is a private domain, accessible over the lock-gates and reserved for the owners of its fifteen plots. Queen's Eyot, near Bray Marina, was bought by Eton College for £1 in 1900, and has for years been used as a weekend retreat and a place of 'contemplation' by Eton schoolboys. Nowadays, however, they may be more likely to go there to watch Sky TV, at least on days when the island is not being hired out for corporate functions and weddings. Part of an estate now owned by the John Lewis Partnership, Formosa Island, near Cookham, is used for management training.

Some eyots are known only for the slightest accidents of history. Thus Friday Island, by Windsor lock, was long the home of Dr Julius Grant, a forensic scientist remembered as the inventor of Marmite. Others live by the historical riddles locked up in their names. In one local theory, Black Boy Islands, near Medmenham, are named after a boy brought back from Sierra Leone by a member of the local gentry. In another, the name derives from the time of Charles II, whose mother is said to have called him 'the black boy' at birth on account of his dark skin.

Others have a history of being devoted to popular entertainment, like Tagg's Island, near Hampton, which for years featured an entertainment complex owned by Fred Karno, the debauched impresario who has been described as the founder of English slapstick comedy. Stan Laurel and Charlie Chaplin performed at the 'Karsino', and Charlie Chaplin visited Tagg's Island shortly before he left England for the United States. In his autobiography, he describes being entertained on Karno's fabulously opulent houseboat, 'The Astoria'.[10] The vessel was festooned with charming coloured lights and, since it was a warm and beautiful evening, the two men sat out on the upper deck for coffee and cigarettes. 'This was the England that could wean me away from any country,' so Chaplin thought as he gazed out over the river. But he had forgotten the tradition of Thames class warfare, for, just at that point, 'a falsetto, foppish voice began screaming hysterically: "Oh, look at my lovely boat, everyone! Look at my lovely boat! And the lights! Ha! Ha! Ha!"'

Looking out, they saw a rowing boat with an upper-class twit in white flannels at the oars and a lady reclining on the back seat: 'The ensemble was like a comic illustration from *Punch*.' Karno leaned over the rail and blew a loud raspberry, and Chaplin took over when this failed to see off the attackers. '"There is only one thing to do," I said, "to be a vulgar as he thinks we are." So I let out a violent flow of Rabelaisian invective, which was so embarrassing for his lady that he quickly moved away.' For Chaplin, this outburst of 'snobbish prejudice' was typical of the 'ever-present class tabulating' that had made England a place that he, as a man of poor and uneducated origins, would do better to leave. As for Fred Karno, trade at his 'Karsino' was all too susceptible to bad English weather, and he went bankrupt in 1926. His only surviving relic near Tagg's Island, 'The Astoria', is now owned by David Gilmour of Pink Floyd and used as a recording studio.

High times at the 'Karsino' on Tagg's Island, 1913. Opened that year, Fred Karno's 'Fun Palace' had a hotel, a ballroom and a stage, but the English weather proved overwhelming.

Monkey Island, near Bray, derives its name from 'Monks Eyot', meaning Monks' Island. Once part of a monastic fishery, the island was solidified and raised against flooding in the seventeenth century, when rubble from the Fire of London was carried upriver and dumped on this and other eyots. The fishing lodge, built for the third Duke of Marlborough in 1723, has since been incorporated into a hotel and inn. Royal parties used to stop for picnics here. When I stayed, I went down to breakfast to find all the other guests talking about Mali, Monterey, and Rio de Janeiro. I was perplexed until I realized that I was perhaps the only guest who wasn't part of an air-crew from nearby Heathrow.

Nowadays, Eel Pie Island is surely the most congenial island on the Thames, and the one most actively devoted to the tradition of freedom more or less under the law. Known as the only inhabited island on the tidal river, it stands a few metres offshore from Twickenham, and is said to derive its name from an eel pie stall that Henry VII used to patronize as he travelled the river to and from Windsor. There is no access for cars, but a little footbridge was built in 1957, an innovation that some inhabitants of this notoriously off-beat island may have been regretting ever since.

Twenty years ago, the writer Norman Shrapnel described Eel Pie as a 'seven-acre social adventure playground' holding out against smart residential development.[11] That description still makes sense today. There are some smart, conventional houses on the island, but the general atmosphere of the place is determined by dwellings which are unmistakably closer to the shack or cabin – plotland structures of the self-built variety that once covered Canvey Island. Norman Shrapnel regretted 'the hash the developers are making out of Eel Pie'. He must have been thinking of the eighteen riverside houses of the 'Aquarius' estate, built on the site of the Eel Pie Hotel after it burned down in 1972. But his dismay has not deterred recent immigrants to the island, including a scriptwriter for *The Bill* who is said by his less well-off neighbours to have paid a fortune for one of those houses.

The local celebrity who most epitomizes the Eel Pie spirit is Trevor Baylis, former professional swimmer and stuntman, and now famous as the inventor who came up with the clockwork radio. This Eel Pie contrivance is not an invention of the kind that might be found upstream. It is not a high-tech

Tokamak, or a super-conducting silicon chip; or a state-of-the-art engine-cooling system for main battle tanks, such as you might find at the factory of Airscrew Howden upstream in Sunbury. Instead, it's a canny contrivance, an ingenious exploitation of existing knowledge presented as a triumph for social rather than merely financial values. Mainland inventors nowadays may congregate on science parks, but Baylis's workplace is not like that at all. Its corridors are public pathways, and its rooms are variously his house, a shed and a couple of lock-up garages known as 'Bum' and 'Wanker' after the words that a passing vandal once scrawled on their doors.

Baylis built his own house in the early seventies, using a plot that formerly accommodated a scout-hut, and bricks that, as other islanders observe with a knowing smile, bear a close resemblance to those of the Aquarius development then being constructed just downstream. The doors open into a small workshop, and a bowl on the living-room table contains what must be the deadest pineapple in the entire world. 'I live in the squalor that suits me,' says Baylis, adding that his is the kind of house where 'if you want a spanner, you're probably sitting on it'.

'We think of people who don't live on the island as having a bit of a problem,' he says. He is well aware that a far larger number of people living on the mainland see little on Eel Pie Island except 'thirty drunks clinging to a mudflat'. But for him Eel Pie is for people who have not been broken by the world, a place of otherness, freedom and untrammelled imagination. To take a term from chess, it's an island devoted to the knight's move.

The Eel Pie Hotel may have been running tea-dances in the twenties, but even then it was finding another role. Indeed, Baylis is in no doubt at all that 'sex was invented on Eel Pie Island'. Traditionally, he suggests, it was a case of 'wives in Twickenham and tarts and strumpets on Eel Pie Island'. In the early days, some of the shacks and cabins were bought by prosperous businessmen, who used to install their mistresses there, and then come and visit them. A few of these 'charming old dears' were still around until quite recently.

By the fifties the Eel Pie Hotel was running jazz and skiffle nights. Baylis remembers women in black with enormous hairdos, skip-jiving in jeans and long sweaters. And it wasn't at all rare to see people going 'all the way' on the

It's not easy to convert the Thames into the Mississippi as Mark Twain described it in *Huckleberry Finn*, but the reclusive 'Raftman', whose floating home and garden is anchored between Twickenham and Richmond, has done as well as anyone.

side of the path. That impression is confirmed by George Melly, who remembers Eel Pie as a 'rural slum' with a permanent cloud of pot smoke hanging over it. As for the hotel, where Melly launched himself as a jazz singer, it was a wonderful dilapidated place that 'might have come straight out of Tennessee Williams': sit on the verandah, imbibe the right stuff, and the Thames melted into the Mississippi for a night.

In those days, the Eel Pie Hotel was owned by a man called Michael Snapper, but its emergence as a musical venue was the work of Arthur Chishall. Still remembered on the island as a 'social researcher', Chishall applied his interest in 'trend-forming groups' to the young people who had nowhere to go and no real sense of identity either. So he persuaded Snapper to help him set up a club called Eelpiland. There were dances and concerts to be sure, but the club also helped people find accommodation, ran educational workshops and courses, and helped some of its members into college. The club survived the transition from trad jazz (star performers included George Melly, Ken Colyer and Chris Barber) to R&B and early rock, attended by Rod Stewart, the Who, Long John Baldry, Georgie Fame and Jeff Beck. The Rolling Stones played there a few times, too; and local legend still recalls them carting their own equipment over the footbridge. The club closed in 1967. Arthur Chishall blames a 'vendetta' run by a local MP, and insists that the club's real offence was not making a noise, or attracting drug-traffickers or under-age drinkers, but 'teaching people to think for themselves – an unforgivable sin'.

Baylis has his laws and sayings to rival the flip-chart axioms of the straightest mainland management consultant. Eel Pie Island is 'not a place to live, but a way to live', he bluffs. And 'Convention is an obstacle to progress'.

Rosa Diaz's house and garden, planted with some of her plastic dolls, on Eel Pie Island.

The latter nostrum is delivered on the path, where we are admiring the garden of Rosa Diaz, a Portuguese resident who has planted the ground with scores of dismembered plastic dolls gathered from Twickenham charity shops.

Further up the same path is a working boat-yard, one of the few that hasn't gone down to residential development on this stretch of the Thames, and beyond that a tangle of charred timbers and burned-out buildings. This, too, was once a boat-yard, but it was converted into studios in the mid-eighties and leased out to a varied company of photographers, artists, leather workers, potters and furniture-makers, etc. Most of these artisans got burned out in 1996 – victims of the second fire to visit the island in its recent history.

There are various signs of recovery in the ashes – studios housed in shacks, a Noah-like ark and, in another case, the metal cabin from a once considerable ship. The first of these structures to catch the eye is an impossibly bright pink shed with an interior which is also a riot of bright pastel colours. This is Rosa

Diaz's studio, and she sits here in her capacity as a costume designer whose varied works have been used for pantomimes, operas, and television advertisements. Throughout these commissions, she is, as she explains, waging her own war against English greyness. Bright colours may at last be infiltrating the average English home, she concedes, but it still takes an undue measure of courage for anyone in this country to step out of their house wearing a bright pink coat.

As is the way in Bohemia, very few of these artisans were insured at the time of the fire, and though some restitution was possible thanks to funds raised through an appeal, the prospect of 'development' looms over their settlement. Soon after the fire, the owner of the burned-out yard declared himself in no position but to sell the land. Half the plot was bought by a consortium led by the one tenant who had been insured; but the remaining half was acquired by a developer who goes by the name of 'Platonic Partnerships'. His involvement worries the islanders who suggest that, even with his hippy-like name and his initial proposal of 'live-in ateliers', there would be nothing to prevent him changing his mind and trying to get this site, which is currently zoned for heavy industrial use, recategorized and dedicated to upmarket residential housing.

For the time being, though, Eel Pie Island remains an alternative Runnymede, an island of DIY democracy, holding out against the powers of 'the mainland'. When occasion demands, the islanders hold a community meeting, says Baylis, and they may also sort out problems during parties in one or other resident's home.

Rosa Diaz confesses that she tends to avoid the 'very tedious' meetings. But Guy Harden, a sculptor in the boat-yard, remarks that people seem to behave better in a close community – you have to live together, which means people control themselves. There's nothing like 'road rage' on Eel Pie Island.

As for the remaining boat-yard, that is run by Edward Leppard. 'It's a living,' he says, before going on to express a proper working-man's doubts about the burned-out Bohemians who hadn't bothered to insure themselves, and then had the nerve to turn round and launch a public appeal. Leppard has a full list of boats awaiting repair at his yard. Yet he, too, feels threatened. The fire opened him up to the prospect of residential development immediately next door. And if that happens, he anticipates that the council will be closing him down within a few months. Boat-yards have to work with the tides, and nobody wants that sort of noise on their doorstep, even if the ship-yard has been there for years. He could make a fortune selling the site for residential development, but, although he volunteers that he may well be looking to sell up before very long, he is determined to resist the mainland tendency to go for the highest price at all cost. He'll take less money, he says, but he is determined to leave a working boat-yard behind him. Counting up the number that have already gone down to residential development in the area, he issues his own Eel Pie edict: 'Nobody is going to pull down a housing estate to make a boat-yard.'

SOUNDING OFF

Mohamed Al Fayed was having a decidedly mixed week when I met him at Craven Cottage, the Thames-side ground of Fulham Football Club. The owner of Harrods had just heard that Jack Straw had turned down his application for British citizenship and, yet, that afternoon Fulham beat Preston N.E., in the final game of a season in which it had won the Championship Trophy for Division Two, and ensured its promotion to the First Division.

The Home Secretary may have his doubts, but Al Fayed is worshipped and revered as a saviour at his football ground, which he bought in 1997, when the club had fallen to the bottom of the Third Division and when it seemed that only its prime riverside site had any value. Instead of selling the ground off for development, as some feared he would, he poured money into the club, hiring Kevin Keegan as manager and launching an extraordinary recovery. A new 26,000-seat stadium is planned, and Al Fayed hopes to see his prodigiously bank-rolled team breaking into the Premier League by the end of the year 2000. Before the match he made his customary 'Victory Walk', wandering around the pitch brandishing the Fulham scarf at the enraptured crowd.

During the second half of the game, I joined Al Fayed in the directors' box where we sat with our backs to the Thames. When I asked him to say a few words about the river, a few metres behind us, he obligingly likened it to the Nile beside which he grew up: it was, he said, a spiritual stream alive with 'the secret of life', a river of vision and, as he was happy to confirm when I prodded him in the direction, of 'liquid history', too. Looking out at the crowd, he remarked that this was the Britain he wanted to belong to: a country of working-class folk who were decent, open-minded and devoted to fair play; and who had already embraced him as one of their own. Insisting that he was 'basically a socialist at heart' who had embarked on his business career with only £500, the scandal-ridden owner of

Harrods then widened his hymn of praise by extolling the virtues of British businessmen, academics, inventors and scientists.

Yet Al Fayed's expression darkened when he got round to 'the people up there, the establishment, the barons'. Suddenly he was raging not so much at the politicians, whom he dismisses merely as manipulated 'dummies' or 'zombies', as at the 'bastard' permanent secretaries, the House of Windsor and the intelligence services; and wrapping them all up together to produce the shadowy power behind the scenes which, he is convinced, murdered his son Dodie and Princess Diana. Margaret Thatcher apparently had surrounded herself with 'crooks and gangsters', but the Queen was even worse. As for Robin Cook, 'I would not appoint him as a butcher behind my counter, or as a doorman.' During the course of this diatribe, Fulham Football Club's saviour described No. 10 Downing Street as 'a night club for arms dealers' and then expressed his hope that 'the masses' who had come out so strongly for Princess Diana, would one day rise up and make this 'trash' disappear.

Al Fayed has his own way of putting the accusation, but the London Thames has certainly heard vehement anti-Parliamentary argument before. Indeed, as a man who once cited a biography of Thomas Paine as the last book he read, Al Fayed might also be able to draw some consolation from the views of Edward Sexby, the Leveller, who, on 29 October 1647, announced that 'any wise, discreet man that hath preserved England is worthy of a voice in the government of it'.

Those words were spoken during the English Civil War in Putney, just across the river from Fulham. The church in which the famous Putney Debates were held has since been wholly rebuilt, but the resounding Biblical cadences of the speech that filled it during those three days in 1647 endure to this day, thanks to the then recently-invented shorthand system of William Clark who, as secretary to the Army Council, recorded the proceedings.

The Putney Debates occurred at a time when the outcome of the English Civil War was still uncertain. In the spring of that year the majority in Parliament had wanted to negotiate a settlement with the King. It proposed disbanding part of Cromwell's New Model Army and sending the rest of it off to assault Ireland. The soldiers had responded by electing Agitators to press for their rights, and there was close contact between the Agitators and the Levellers, for whom the army was the representative of the people of God in England.

The Agitators made the running for several months. It was apparently on their orders that the otherwise anonymous Cornet Joyce and his troop arrested Charles I in June 1647. And at the meetings in Putney church, which began on 28 October, they presented the Army Council with the Levellers' proposed 'Agreement of the People'. The Agreement outlined a new republican constitution in which parliament would be elected every two years, and there would be no place for either the King or the House of Lords. The Agitators repudiated the present Parliament as a 'rotten beamed' edifice, full of 'rotten members', and proposed a new democratic system of Parliamentary representation. As one of them put it, 'I think the poorest he that is in England has a life to live as the greatest he; and therefore truly, sir, I think it is clear, that every man that is to live under a government ought first by his own consent to put himself under that government.'

There was a great argument whether democracy should rest on property, as both Cromwell and Commissary-General Henry Ireton were inclined to insist. Speaking for the unpropertied who had fought 'to recover our birthrights and privileges as Englishmen', the Agitators rejected this as 'the old law of England and that which enslaves the people of England'. These debates did not lead to the national renewal envisaged by the Levellers. Charles I escaped from custody on 11 November, and army discipline was reinstated. The Levellers' cause broke out in fitful mutinies after that, but was finally crushed at Burford, in the Cotswolds, in May 1649.

Mohamed Al Fayed and the Levellers united in contempt for the Westminster establishment... This is an odd coincidence to find at the start of the London river, but the London Thames remains a visionary stream to this day, even if, in the new Labour metropolis, PR and 'spin' do often seem to have replaced the Levellers' redeeming politics of 'delivering the kingdom'.

A LABOUR PEER TAKES TO THE WATER

The Thames at Westminster can rarely have seemed wider than it did in the 1980s when Capitalism and Socialism glared at each other from the opposed banks while a steadily increasing number of pleasure-boats sailed up and down between the two. Margaret Thatcher presided over the Houses of Parliament on the north bank, and Ken Livingstone's chaotic but generally life-enhancing Greater London Council sat opposite on the south bank in County Hall: 'I never liked it much,' so Ken Livingstone said of his vast command-bunker in the *Daily Mirror* in 1987, 'it's a bit Stalinist, one of those buildings designed to intimidate people. But when we filled it with black, lesbian, environmentalist and peace groups, it made it less harsh, more human.'

As if to express Margaret Thatcher's disgust at these antics across the water, the Houses of Parliament were thoroughly restored in those years: cleansed, regilded and polished up to a high symbolic shine. Livingstone's GLC also exploited the theatrical possibilities of County Hall, draping it with a large red banner announcing the number of unemployed in London. This gesture made County Hall look like a municipal building in some dire Soviet bloc country, and it was all too much for the ruling Tory politicians, who sat on the terrace of the Palace of

The staff at County Hall on the last day of the Greater London Council, 31 March 1986.

Lord Noel-Buxton sets out to prove that hereditary peers really could serve the national interest.

Westminster, gazing back at that lurid banner across Westminster Bridge and dreaming of the abolition of the GLC.

The water was wide in those days, but not nearly so wide as it must have appeared to Rufus Noel-Buxton, a gentleman whose photograph appeared in the *Illustrated London News* on 5 April 1952. The picture shows a stooped figure wading into the Thames from the steps immediately upstream from Westminster Bridge. The water is already up to his thighs and it must have been cold, too, for there is an apprehensive hesitancy in his stride. Big Ben and the Palace of Westminster loom up from the far bank in stately splendour, and the man in the water is attended by an official-looking launch with a prominently displayed flag, which one feels to be red, even though the picture is in black and white.

The man in the Thames was Rufus Noel-Buxton, the second Baron of Aylsham, one of the most original of the hereditary peers who, over the course of the twentieth century, have stepped out of the House of Lords in search of a modern role.

A month or so previously, he had left the Liberal Party in order to become, in his own words, 'a mild but far from negative' member of the Labour Party. This change of allegiance had actually been something of a homecoming. For, despite the fact that he had entered the Lords as a Liberal in 1948, the second Baron of Aylsham was actually a representative of Old Labour: not the post-war variety associated with hard statism and strong Soviet sympathies, but an older version that was attended by a powerfully aristocratic background and, in the beginning at least, a considerable fortune in the bank.

For the press, the fluvial perambulation of this 'tall and rufous' Baron was a diverting episode of light relief at a time when the news was dominated by the ongoing Korean war. But Lord Noel-Buxton actually had his own serious purpose in mind. He had studied the route followed by the oldest section of the Roman Road called Watling Street as it came up from Canterbury to London, and concluded that, since the Romans had been 'geometrically minded' in their assault on the Thames marshland, one could deduce where they crossed the Thames by extending the line of Watling Street into London. Having completed this operation, presumably with the help of an Ordnance Survey map and a ruler, he decided that the Romans must have forded the Thames at Westminster.

So, on the morning of Tuesday, 25 March 1952, this newly re-Labourized peer set out to prove his theory by walking down the embankment steps by St Thomas's Hospital. Having sampled the water with what an American paper, the *Hartford Courant*, called 'a tentative toe', he waded into the Thames 'casually clad' in flannels, gym shoes, a blue shirt and a green jersey.

The public had been well prepared for the event, and many people joined the reporters who were peering out over the parapet of Westminster Bridge to watch the progress of this peer. Lord Noel-Buxton knew that, thanks to the embankment built by Sir Joseph Bazalgette in the 1870s, which had both narrowed and hastened the flow of the river, the water would be deeper than in Roman times. But he was an experienced forder of rivers, and enjoyed trying to stand in fast water – 'Good exercise' as he called it, although not of a variety that has yet been simulated at the exclusive spa and gym which now operates in the upper floors of the GLC's old haunt at County Hall. He expected to encounter one or two 'potholes', where he might have to swim, but had chosen a very low tide and estimated that the water would be no deeper than 5 feet 3 inches, which should not pose too much of a problem, since he himself was 6 feet 3 inches tall.

According to the *Manchester Guardian*, Lord Noel-Buxton made it almost to the second pier of Westminster Bridge but then 'down he went'. It was only by swimming strenuously that he reached the steps at the Palace of Westminster, where the Speaker was waiting, perhaps a little anxiously, to receive him. The journey had taken seventeen minutes, and prompted the frozen peer to admit that 'There was much more water than I expected'. He later attributed his failure to the fact that it must have been raining 'pretty freely' in the Cotswolds.

The Times counted the fact that Noel-Buxton's 'wade turned into a swim' as a victory for the river, which had recently been humiliated by 'too much fun and games' – crossed by a tight-rope artist and another gentleman who somehow contrived to 'walk' over at Chelsea. Yet in England discontent is often expressed as eccentricity, and there can be no doubt that, in his own muddy way, Noel-Buxton was actually a protest marcher stepping out against the Spirit of the Age. As a 'poetical archaeologist' who once spoke of 'doing' rivers, he was wading against the idea that history itself no longer counted.[1] He was wading against clock time ('There were no Minutes in the Ice Age'), and the endless spread of housing and the 'submergence of an island under brick, which precedes the submergence of the island under water'. A 'romantic idealist' who 'would like to see more green in England', he had been disappointed, during the brief period when he had an editorial job on *Farmers Weekly*, to find that it was merely a trade journal, and not really interested in 'the aesthetic, rural-radical point of view'. So here he was trying to recover a sense of the wilderness in London itself. His river walk was an attempt to restore the memory of 'London the Immortal' against the drabness of contemporary Tottenham Court Road. Eccentric or not, it was an act of defiance, intended to 'get the word Ford into print, not meaning a Ford car'.

A former BBC radio producer, the 'Westminster Wader' likened his unconventional way of seeing to a film in which two cameras were working at once.

Through Camera One, he saw the world just as it appeared to everyone else gathered on Westminster Bridge. There was the embankment, the double-decker buses, and Sir Charles Barry's Palace of Westminster, the vast neo-Gothic building erected after the old Houses of Parliament had been destroyed by fire in 1834. Noel-Buxton knew the entire length of this building well enough. For a while,

indeed, he had overlapped there with his mother, Lucy Edith, who was in the Commons as Labour MP for Norwich, and used to speak about 'Poor old Rufie at the sinking end of the ship'.

Admirers of British democracy may be inclined to dwell on the neo-Gothic grandeur of this palace which dresses the British state in medieval ancientry. Noel-Buxton was well aware of this, but he surely also knew that the stately encrustations on the exterior of the Palace of Westminster actually served to disguise a formidable hot-air machine.

The critics of the British state who like to point this out are not just referring to the windbaggery that afflicts so much parliamentary debate.[2] For while Barry's building may have been designed to symbolize British

The Palace of Westminster, looking down on 'the sinking end of the ship'.

government, it also set out to tackle the terrible stench that had often attended parliamentary business in the previous building. This was blamed variously on nearby glue and bone-meal factories, but the polluted river was at the root of the problem.

Determined to avoid this problem in the new building, some Members had attended a conference of the British Association for the Advancement of Science in Edinburgh, and it was here that they met David Boswell Reid, a strange and autocratic figure who had developed his own specialist interest in the modern science of ventilation. Employed to design a heating and ventilation system for the new Palace of Westminster, Reid planned a system that would use great furnaces to heat air, and then distribute it through the building by means of an elaborate system of ducts and flues hidden behind Sir Charles Barry's neo-Gothic façade.

This attempt to freshen the stinking passages of British democracy was not without its difficulties. Reid's system threatened to take up a third of the space needed inside the building, and would, according to one estimate, have required a staff of sixteen to operate it properly. Reid came to be known as 'Aerial Guy Fawkes' as it emerged that his elaborate hot-air machine would also require large amounts of fire-proofing. Indeed, before he was sacked, Reid went considerably further in his recommendations for the new building: 'Now my notion of things is, that there should be nothing but metallic ceilings, metallic roofs, metallic floors, metallic tables, metallic chairs.'

Yet if Noel-Buxton brought some awareness of this history to the Palace of Westminster as it appeared through Camera One, he was more at home with Camera Two, which kept throwing up pictures from a considerably more ancient past. Indeed, as he waded towards it, Sir Charles Barry's grand building kept giving way to reveal the marsh that had once been here, and which the Saxons had known as Thorney: a wet and muddy place of bramble, white thorn and bitterns – 'abhorrent to all except perhaps those of the wild-fowling temperament'. Some way into his swim he even counted up the plants that once grew at Westminster, from the smooth-headed bustard poppy to Mr Doddy's water-reed grass.

As he pressed on through that momentarily reactivated old ford (he imagined 'paving stones under feet of silt and gravel'), Noel-Buxton saw old Westminster coming to life right in front of him. No sooner had he glimpsed the primeval swamp that had been Offa's nightmare, than the Palace of Canute suddenly materialized where the western part of the House of Lords now stands. He then watched as the little monastery built by the Saxons in the seventh century was expanded by Edward in the tenth century to make Westminster Abbey, complete with the Chapter House where the Commons first sat.

Noel-Buxton enjoyed these reactivated visions of ancient Westminster, and yet he was in no doubt that they reflected morbidity in the present, revealing that the House of Lords especially lacked sufficient reality to resist the usurping ghosts that rose up at it from the river. Aware that the House of Lords had already lost its gravitational force to the Commons, he could see the eastern end of the Palace see-sawing up into the air and then crashing down into the 'militant mud'. He was another Thames catastrophist: more lordly than the Richard Jefferies of *After London*, but quite aware that he was by no means the first person to see London in this extreme way. Indeed, he placed his own vision of tottering Westminster in the tradition of Lord Macaulay who, while writing about the endurance of the Roman Catholic Church in the 1840s, had imagined a traveller from New Zealand visiting London to find 'a vast solitude' and taking his stand on the broken arch of London bridge to sketch the ruins of St Paul's.[3]

A few years after that Westminster crossing, the novelist Evelyn Waugh described Rufus Noel-Buxton in the most insulting terms, claiming that he had turned up uninvited on his Gloucestershire door step with a disreputable female reporter from the *Daily Express*, a ridiculous figure who had compounded this breach of etiquette by saying, 'I'm not on business. I am a member of the House of Lords.'[4] Noel-Buxton's unwelcome appearance led Waugh to suggest that the men like Rufus's father, the former Labour Minister of Agriculture, who had been 'put into ermine' by Ramsay Macdonald, believed that 'the order that they were entering was doomed'. But the House of Lords had out-lasted them, and their successors were left as 'orphans of the storm that blew itself out'. The result was Rufus Noel-Buxton, a new and utterly pointless kind of 'predatory peer', who was only good for 'paddling in rivers' or serving as a 'tout for television'.

Noel-Buxton repudiated these insults, and yet, in *Westminster Wader*, he too described his peerage as an imprisoning burden, a cruel joke that stood between him and his fellow humanity. As one who was 'nearly bankrupt', he admitted to sometimes wishing that hereditary peers were paid – 'I mean, paid if we turn up'. Yet he knew that the House of Lords was a floundering anachronism in the modern age. His Thames crossing was actually an attempt to prove that, rather than sinking beneath 'the tide of this democracy', a reformed hereditary chamber just might be useful once again. He waded with this hope in mind – imagining the House of Lords transformed into a place of 'clear thinking' which offered 'a little breathing space from the world of affairs'. He imagined the hereditary peer not as a landed baron or a party-political drone, but as an enlightened debater of such topics as 'the Reorganisation of Society', who would help the unaccustomed public become interested in such arcane but essential quandaries as 'Has the past of a place got the power to save its present?'

The House of Lords has had its moments since then, but the recommended transformations were avoided. As for the Lord Noel-Buxtons, they were destined to continue in their sad decline, dragging what Rufus once called the 'noose of heredity' behind them as they staggered on through the years. Rufus drank himself into an early grave, but this sad fact should not obscure the relevance of his most distinguished act.

For the Westminster Wader was surely trying to warn his fellow hereditary peers that the end was coming half a century before Tony Blair ennobled Melvyn Bragg and Margaret Jay, and ordered them into the Lords' tea-room to tell these sad human relics that the game was finally up… Perhaps some did see Noel-Buxton's fluvial perambulation as an exemplary project designed to indicate the kind of behaviour a hereditary peer might profitably adopt in the television age. But if posterity deigns to remember Rufus Noel-Buxton's promenade at all, it will not be because the House of Lords woke up to this challenge. Instead, it will see Rufus Noel-Buxton pushing forward through the water in dire anticipation of the final redundancy that would mark the millennium for the hereditary peers. As he put it in *Westminster Wader*, 'you'll see all the peers wading for their lives before long'.

ST PAUL'S FROM COIN STREET

When it comes to 'delivering the kingdom' nowadays, one of the more promising places on the London river is a thirteen-acre stretch of land on the south bank between Waterloo and Blackfriars Bridge. In the early eighties, the area around Coin Street became notorious as a battleground on which people fought it out with property, and actually won. Assisted latterly by Ken Livingstone's GLC, local residents formed the Coin Street Action Group and then set about seeing off the developers bent on displacing them: first Gerald Ronson's Heron Corporation, which planned to build a multi-storey hotel on the site, and then Stuart Lipton of Greycoats who proposed a twenty-storey office block designed by Richard

Rogers. This development would effectively have sealed off the river behind a glassy monolith that the Coin Street agitators denounced as 'the Berlin Wall'. As for Richard Rogers, the fact that he is now known as 'Lord Rogers of Riverside', causes smiles to appear on the faces of those who once fought him off as 'the Cossack of Coin Street'.

When the residents finally took possession from the GLC in 1984, the eight assembled sites consisted of various derelict wharves and warehouses, and the old Eldorado ice-cream factory, too. Designed by the local authority architects, the first phase of community housing at Coin Street is a dull-looking low-density development of two-storey terraces that would seem more at home in a suburb. But access to the river was opened too, creating a park and a riverside walk. Architectural competitions ensured that the housing was greatly improved by the second phase, especially in the award-winning Palm Housing Co-op development.

St Paul's viewed from Coin Street, with Oxo Tower Wharf to the right.

The most recent achievement is the refurbishment of the OXO Tower Wharf. Once used to make OXO and latterly also the long tubular eggs that stretch out through the middle of industrial pork pies, this meat warehouse has been rescued from dereliction and converted to an unusual variety of uses. There are workshops and design studios, along with numerous residential flats; and the 'posh restaurant' on the top floor is run by Harvey Nichols. Speaking for Coin Street Community Builders, Louise King is pleased to point out that the amount a banker, politician or media mogul might spend on lunch in the restaurant would probably cover a whole week's rent in one of the magnificently appointed riverside flats below. This does not make the restaurant astronomically expensive by London standards, for, despite their magnificent location, all the flats in OXO Tower Wharf are actually used as co-operatively-managed low-rent social housing.

The Coin Street agitators did not just defend their community from displacement by property barons. In 1987, Coin Street was praised by Jules Lubbock, then the architecture critic of the *New Statesman*, for opening up a 'wonderful new public view' downstream along the river to St Paul's Cathedral. The view of Wren's great classical building had been closed by wharves and warehouses for some 200 years, and would have been lost to the public had the money-men had their way. St Paul's had been 'the very symbol of the British people in the face of Nazism', but was 'shamefully mutilated' by the developers who had thrown up mediocre office towers all around it in the post-war years. By restoring this view to the public, the people who now trade as Coin Street Community Builders had carried out a great act of public redress.

Jules Lubbock viewed St Paul's from the Coin Street's riverside garden, but an even more spectacular view is now provided by the public viewing gallery on the eighth floor of the refurbished OXO Tower Wharf. Some people are so fond of this new amenity that they arrive with carefully prepared picnics, which can hardly be what Harvey Nichols expected. The gallery is also a perfect vantage point from which to consider the curious symbolic career of Wren's dome over the last fifty or so years. St Paul's has a wonderful sense of timelessness about it, but when viewed with an eye for its modern significance, Wren's dome starts 'moving about' every bit as strangely as the Palace of Westminster did for Rufus Noel-Buxton.

For Robert Byron, who wrote a guide for London Transport in 1937, the dome of St Paul's was a monument not just to its architect Sir Christopher Wren, but to 'that bold enquiring and experimental spirit which gave birth to the Royal Society, and, a century later, to England's lead over Europe in the Industrial Revolution'.[5] An emblem of reason and science, the dome was the symbolic hub of a British empire that consisted not of conquered territories but of free peoples 'united by a common will to liberty'.

That association with liberty and reason was deepened during the Second World War. Herbert Mason's famous picture, printed in the *Daily Mail* on 31 December 1940, showed the unbroken dome of St Paul's looming through the fire and smoke of the blitz – a symbol of democratic values holding out against total-itarian tyranny, and of reason enduring through the irrational deluge. Indeed, the documentary film-maker Humphrey Jennings even wrote a poem in which he imagined the head of Charles Darwin superimposed over Wren's dome.

Once the bombing was over, however, St Paul's was soon being cherished in opposition to the commercial and municipal development springing up on all sides of it. Mournful figures started measuring the dome of St Paul's against the present, and muttering that post-war redevelopment (and it quickly came to make little difference whether this was carried out for profit or in an idealistic spirit of social reform) was actually doing more damage to London than the Nazi bombers had ever done.

John Betjeman was one of the first to harness old paintings of St Paul's to this new crusade. In a poem, 'Meditation on a Constable Picture', published in the 1970s, he hailed the 'steeple surrounded' dome of St Paul's, and commended the absence of modern 'slabs' of the sort that had since been thrown up around it. Then, in 'City of Towers', an influential television documentary of 1978, Christopher Booker invoked Canaletto as well as Constable, using their pictures of St Paul's to condemn the high-rise architecture of the post-war welfare state.

By the 1980s, the dome of St Paul's had become a pivotal image for those who, not content with redeclaring the memory of the Second World War against the post-war peace, dreamed of undoing the damage. In 1987, Theo Crosby, an architect and partner in the Pentagram design consultancy, proposed that London should be both revived and extended along two river-based 'axes' derived from classical views of St Paul's Cathedral: 'the Canaletto Axis', which reached from the terrace of Somerset House, and 'the Turner Axis' which followed that great painter's eye down onto St Paul's from Greenwich. But it was Prince Charles who really put the seal on this tendency, and he did it with the assistance of his architectural adviser Jules Lubbock.

In December 1987, only a few weeks after Lubbock had praised the view of St Paul's from Coin Street, Prince Charles delivered the notorious Mansion House speech in which he described St Paul's as London's 'spiritual centre', and then, with the help of Canaletto, excoriated the 'jostling scrum' of mediocre office buildings now surrounding it. Charles then went on to incorporate the lament for

Canaletto, 'The Thames from the Terrace of Somerset House looking downstream towards St Paul's', c.1750.

St Paul's into *A Vision of Britain*. To begin with, that 'Vision' was a television programme and book featuring Canaletto, Turner and also Christopher Booker, who joined Charles as he sailed down the London Thames denigrating the modern buildings in televisual sound-bites. A year or so later, in 1989, the 'Vision' was converted into an exhibition at the Victoria and Albert Museum, complete with a Saatchi and Saatchi poster which announced, 'In 1945, the Luftwaffe stopped bombing London. Two years later the blitz began.'

Prince Charles articulated genuine public concern when he came to the relief of St Paul's, but the debate that followed degenerated into a futile battle between architectural styles. For Charles and his followers, 'delivering the kingdom' meant getting rid of modernism, returning to the classical orders as espoused by new

Turner, 'London from Greenwich Park', exhibited 1809.

stately-home architects such as Quinlan Terry, and denigrating the post-war social reformers whose New Jerusalem had somehow turned into a hideous collection of system-built tower blocks. 'Vision' became a wholly architectural quality, and the designers of the post-war welfare state became guilty people, who, in Theo Crosby's words, had been too preoccupied by '"useful" short term strategies' like schools and hospitals, when they should have been building obelisks and classical monuments instead.

So we should be grateful to the Coin Street Community Builders, not just for insisting that we look at St Paul's from a new point of view, but for putting social priorities before questions of style and proving that choice riverside flats can be inhabited by fire-fighters, shop-workers and bus-drivers: the kind of people, as the

Coin Street Community Builders put it with a certain pride, 'who keep the city working'.

BODIES IN THE RIVER

A narrow gap between iron and stone: that is how Charles Dickens described the distance between Southwark Bridge and London Bridge in the opening chapter of *Our Mutual Friend*. And it was in this small stretch of the London river that he placed a small boat with two people in it: Gaffer Hexam, a ragged, grizzled fellow with matted hair and no hat, and a nineteen-year-old girl called Lizzie, who rowed with a pair of sculls. The tide is receding, and the pair are scanning the river, searching out the places where floating objects might be lodged: moorings, pontoons made of floating logs, the piers of Southwark Bridge. In the boat is the body of a man they've fished out of the water. Gaffer Hexam takes the coins out of his pocket easily enough, and then, as they head back towards Rotherhithe with their cargo, these ghoulish scavengers draw close to another boat and engage in a heated argument with Gaffer Hexam's estranged partner in trade. The dispute concerns the morality, or otherwise, of taking money from a live man and a dead one: the latter alone being an action that Gaffer Hexam will tolerate: 'Has a dead man any use for money?'

That short length of the river is only a tiny part of the wider view of St Paul's from the top of OXO Tower Wharf. Yet 130 years later it has the power to disconcert Jonathan Phang, who recalls keeping his back to the river when he visited Harvey Nichols: 'Don't get me wrong,' he says, 'I love views, but that is not one I want to enjoy.'

If Phang is likely to be struck by a disagreeable 'feeling like vertigo' whenever he drives over the London river, this is entirely because of the disaster that occurred on the *Marchioness*, a pleasure cruiser which had been hired for the twenty-sixth birthday party of his friend Antonio Vasconcellos. The vessel was coming downstream through the bridge when she was rammed and sunk by the *Bowbelle*, a 1500-ton dredger which had been involved in more than half of the eighteen serious incidents that had occurred on the Thames over the previous twenty years. There were 131 passengers on the *Marchioness*, and their average age was twenty-five. Fifty-one died, including Antonio Vasconcellos and his brother Domingos.

Phang was among the party-goers who found themselves swimming for their lives in the 'horrible dirty water' of a Thames that 'seems a lot wider when you're in it'. He was there for some fifteen minutes, while the police rescue-launches roared past heading for the wrong bridge. The London Thames may seem placid enough when viewed from a bridge, but when you are swimming, you realize the strength of its currents and eddies. There was nothing to grip on to even if you could get to the bridge piers or the embanked walls. Phang found a wooden raft, from which he was eventually hauled aboard another pleasure boat, but many people who had managed to jump off the *Marchioness* drowned after swimming for as long as they could.

Later that day, Margaret Thatcher, who had just flown back from holiday in Austria, came downriver on a police launch to inspect the accident site. She was on the BBC News that night, regretting the sinking as 'a tragedy really of the first order', and also speculating about the wave of disaster and accidents that, as Phang himself observes, seem in some way to have defined the closing years of Thatcherism. The *Herald of Free Enterprise* had recently sunk at Zeebrugge, and the roster also includes the fire at King's Cross, Lockerbie, the Clapham train crash and the Hillsborough Stadium. Some of Thatcher's opponents saw a kind of Nemesis in this accumulation of catastrophes, as if they showed the furies unleashed by a government devoted to deregulation. The Marine Accident Investigators would lend some support to that view when it reported on the *Marchioness* disaster seven months later, criticizing the Department of Transport for failing to introduce adequate safety measures to govern vessels on the river. But on the day itself, Margaret Thatcher offered her own idiosyncratic inter- pretation: 'Is it that we now know more of every single disaster? Is it perhaps that the standard of living is higher and more people go out and do these things than ever before? Possibly a combination of the two.'

At the time, Jonathan Phang was in no position to notice the press response. After a week in hospital, he went home to his flat, where he had to clear away the table at which he had entertained his friends before heading off to join the party on the *Marchioness* at 1 a.m. There was nothing to return to in his office either, since all the employees of his small photographic agency had died in the accident. Yet it soon became clear that the *Marchioness* was going to be the disaster that failed really to touch the nation. A public appeal was launched, but it only raised a few thousand pounds, an utterly derisory figure when compared with the millions the people of Liverpool mustered after Hillsborough.

Perhaps, as Phang suggests, this was because there was no media footage: the collision happened in the middle of the night, and the cameras were left with a few distressed survivors coming out of hospital or a momentary shot of the crushed *Marchioness* being lifted from the river bed. Lack of media visibility may have been one cause, yet the poor public response was also conditioned by the way the disaster was perceived. The reports focused on the champagne-sipping fashion-models from the Synchro agency, creating a picture of 'the beautiful people' that appealed to the country's then exacerbated suspicion of metropolitan excess.

The *Marchioness* became a 'disco boat', and the 'night of pleasure' that Phang had organized was widely rendered as a yuppie fling. In reality, the party was attended by a much wider range of people – staff, parents of friends, people Vasconcellos had known at university – but their story never came through. This was the worst disaster to afflict the Thames since the sinking of the *Princess Alice*, a paddle-steamer that collided with a collier in Gallions Reach one night in 1878 and went down with approaching 700 passengers. But it became something of a non-event.

As Phang says, the government seemed to do as little as possible, discounting the possibility of a public inquiry with a speed that left him and other survivors infuriated. As for the thought that the state might have assisted those who had to ship the bodies of their loved ones home, perhaps to Canada or Florida, the attitude was apparently Dickensian: 'Has a dead man any use for money?'

The disaster was not so much as mentioned either in the Queen's Speech for 1989, or in the official video of the year's events. The Thames is bound to be much busier as the riverbuses start servicing the Millennium Dome, but many concerned with its safety worry that the lessons of the *Marchioness* disaster have yet to be learned. The *Bowbelle*'s captain had drunk 5 pints earlier in the day, but a breathalyser test after the disaster proved negative. And, as Jonathan Phang points out, there is still no law to prevent the captain of a dredger, or any other vessel on the Thames, from setting sail while as drunk as a lord.

THE DOCKS

'Out of the strong came forth sweetness.' The biblical legend of bees making honey in the carcass of a lion killed by Samson can still be read on every tin of Lyle's Golden Syrup. It is also carved into the Portland stone of the Tate & Lyle building, albeit the old one called Plaistow Wharf rather than the steaming

complex of tubes, pipes and tanks which stands just downstream on the north bank at Silvertown. England's abiding taste for sweetness is not in question, but the strength that remade the Port of London in modern times came not from a lion, dead, British or otherwise, but from slaves working on sugar plantations in the West Indies.

By the eighteenth century, London was the greatest port in the world, and, in the words of one historian, 'an object of bewilder-

Samuel Scott, 'Coalship on the Thames near Deptford', c.1760.

ment and admiration to all'.[6] J.H. Meister was among the foreign observers who were amazed by the sight of London's river. He urged visitors to

> take boat to go down the Thames, and see the bosom of that noble river bearing thousands and thousands of vessels, some sailing up or down, going or coming from every part of the world, and others moored in five or six tiers as closely to each other as it is possible for them to be; you will then confess that you have beheld nothing that can give you a stronger idea of the noble and happy effects of human industry.

Though marvellous to look at, that crowded river was a frustrating place for the ship-owners, who had to wait for room on the north bank's 'legal quays', most of which had been established in the sixteenth century, or at the more recent 'sufferance wharves' on the south bank. By the 1790s, the congestion was such that there would often be well over 3000 craft moving over a reach of the river that was only 2.5 miles long – perhaps 2000 of them being barges in use as warehouses. The Upper Pool, between London Bridge and the area where Tower Bridge now stands, had moorings for no more than 545 ships, but there would be nearly 800 crowded into it. Vessels were getting damaged and locked in; and the situation was aggravated by silting, which meant that ships were often grounded at low tide, and also by the seasonal trade with its irregular arrivals and 'prolonged occupation of moorings'. In cold winters, ships were even threatened by considerable icebergs, drifting down from above London Bridge.

The ship-owners had long been interested in improving the situation, but were thwarted by the wharfingers, who were reluctant to lose their monopoly of the unenlarged quays. So ships had to wait up to six weeks before discharging their cargoes. Often they would be abandoned by their senior officers and left in the unreliable hands of their labourers. There was extensive pilfering once goods were landed, but much was also lost to 'water-thieves', some of whom moved among the waiting ships in 'Bum-Boats': pretending to sell liquor to sailors and labourers, they actually cut and stole cords, cables and buoys from the ships, and generally pillaged as they went.

This lawless bonanza was closely investigated by Patrick Colquhoun, the magistrate of Queen Square Police Court.[7] He calculated that every ship in the port lost ten hundredweight of sugar per day during the period of discharge. He also insisted that nine-tenths of the pilfering was done by sailors, lumpers, watchmen and others employed in the unloading, and often with the connivance of revenue officers, especially those of the supernumerary kind known as 'glutmen' who were employed on a more casual basis than the regular officers and who themselves spoke about 'making hay while the sun shone'.

In Colquhoun's account, labourers involved in discharging West India ships would fill their hats, pockets and even breeches with sugar. Some of these 'aquatic plunderers' wore 'a thin sack suspended by strings from the shoulders and placed

Opposite
The working river, as photographed by Vernon Richards in the 1950s.

under a waistcoat' – an apparatus that had the advantage of looking like a natural 'protuberance of the belly' even when holding many pounds of sugar. Scullers would row alongside discharging ships, catching all sorts of portable objects (sacks of flour, barrels of rum, kegs of tamarinds) as they flew out of the port-holes, while yet another class of thief would be busy stealing the 'tackle and apparel' of ships rather than their cargo. There were 'gentleman plunderers', too: dealers in spirits or keepers of hemp shops and timber yards who would sail up to discharging ships when they were unattended at night, and then set to work with specially designed 'cranes' which enabled them to suck rum and other liquors off into bladders that might hold anything from two to six gallons.

It may have been in the West India merchants' interests to exaggerate the extent of this pilferage, but there can be little doubt that the sugary fruits of slavery were widely perceived as fair game. In Colquhoun's view, river-plundering had undermined 'the moral principle' to the point where it was 'totally destroyed among a vast body of the lower ranks of the people'. The pilferers 'consider it as a kind of right which attaches to their situation, to plunder wherever an opportunity offers'.

It was not until 1798 that the West India merchants set up a seriously equipped Marine Police Establishment, based at No. 259 Wapping New Stairs. The new force, which had been proposed by Patrick Colquhoun, included a 'Preventive Department' of men acting on detailed written instructions, which were full of dire warnings against corruption. These armed constables patrolled the river and acted as watchmen on board discharging ships. The West India merchants also took steps to create a more disciplined labour force – adopting Colquhoun's scheme for registering and approving lumpers co-ordinated through the Marine Police Establishment office. Master-lumpers were bound by oath, and given an agreed wage, and all labourers had to work in approved clothing ('no Frocks, Trowsers, Jemmies, Pouches, or Bags'), in which filched goods could not easily be hidden.

It is said that the new police officers in Wapping once had to use firearms against an attacking mob of coal-heavers and labourers but, for the ship owners at least, the creation of the Marine Police Establishment certainly changed the river to their advantage. In 1799 a private dock company found that where it had previously taken ten bags of copper nails and 1600 sheets of copper to re-sheathe a ship, the same job could now be done with seven bags of nails and 1480 sheets. Likewise, losses to members of the West India Company fell to a fifth of previous levels.

The privately-sponsored Marine Police Establishment at Wapping was converted into a public institution known as the Thames Police Office in 1800: 'a constantly moving Police on the River', as it would be called, and one that was granted sweeping powers both of arrest and of registration. By 1816, it was being said that the river, for so long infested with crime, had become 'as smooth as a mill-pond'.

The disciplining of the Port of London was partly a matter of law enforcement, but another innovation was involved, too. The case for building secure wet docks was first made in 1793 when William Vaughan, an advocate of free trade, argued for the establishment of such a system at St Katharine's Church, Wapping, the Isle of Dogs and Rotherhithe. A House of Commons Committee reported on the options in 1796, and the West India Docks on the Isle of Dogs were the first new facility to be built under the new Dock Act of 1799. It was to be surrounded by a wall 30 feet high and a ditch of water 12 feet wide and 6 feet deep; and it was initially stipulated that there were to be no buildings within 100 yards of the wall. Opened by the Prime Minister, Henry Addington, in 1802, London's first wet dock was symbolically entered: first by a ship named the *Henry Addington*, which was adorned with all the flags of the world, and then by a working vessel called *The Echo*, laden with sugar.

A whole series of wet docks were created in the nineteenth century. London Docks, which included Tobacco Dock at Wapping, opened in 1805. The East India Dock at Blackwall was built at about the same time, as were the original Surrey Docks in Rotherhithe on the south bank. St Katharine's Dock, the highest on the Thames, was built in the 1820s; and Poplar Dock, formerly a reservoir for the West India Dock, was created to accommodate larger iron ships in 1850. The (Royal) Victoria Dock came later, as did the Royal Albert Dock, which opened in the 1870s, and the King George V Dock, which was begun in 1912.

The construction and improvement of the working river continued through the early twentieth century. Goodhart-Rendel's building at Hay's Wharf in

Bermondsey dates from 1929, and the vast complex of warehouses at Gun Wharves, around the tube station in Wapping, date from the 1930s. But the main event of the later twentieth-century event was closure, which began in the sixties, and has since overtaken all the wet docks above Tilbury.

WAPPING AND LIMEHOUSE: Loft-Living in Hades

Load … unload! that was all! Period! and that's that! …
Dockers! Dockers! That was all! … Commercial or war goods …
No other job! That was what their destiny was like! … They
wouldn't have changed it for anything in the world.

Louis-Ferdinand Céline

The French doctor and novelist Louis-Ferdinand Céline may have underestimated the dockers' will to change, but he still provided one of the most atmospheric descriptions of the London docks as they were in their heyday. Written in occupied France in the early forties, his novel, *Guignol's Band*, is largely based on his own experiences in London during the First World War.

A young man who had already been wounded at the front, Céline had come to London more or less convalescent in 1915 and lodged at 71 Gower Street in Bloomsbury. During the day he worked for the passport office, interviewing Mata Hari among other less exotic applicants. At night he would search out young ballerinas, whose company he is said to have enjoyed in pairs, or head east for the docks: a speedy teetotaller who could be found shaking his medals in pubs around the London Hospital to raise drinks for his friends of the moment.

In *Guignol's Band*, Céline describes stepping out of Wapping underground station into a damp world of tarry fog and little houses, which stretch out along their narrow streets 'like weekdays'. A modest beginning, perhaps, but to approach the docks in this writer's company is like walking into an earthquake:

After the strings of houses, after the unvarying streets
through which I gently accompany you, the walls rise
up…the warehouses, all-brick giant ramparts… Treasure

cliffs!…monster ships…phantasmagoric storehouses, citadels
of merchandise, mountains of tanned goatskins enough to
stink all the way to Kamchatka! Forest of mahogany in
thousands of piles, tied up like asparagus, in pyramids, miles
of materials!…rugs enough to cover the Moon, the whole
world…all the floors in the Universe!… Enough sponges to
dry up the Thames! What quantities!… Enough wool to
smother Europe beneath heaps of cuddly warmth… Herrings
to fill the seas!… Himalayas of powdered sugar…Matches to
fry the poles!… Enormous avalanches of pepper, enough to
make the Seven floods sneeze!…

Similarly exuberant memories are still to be found wherever people who grew
up in the docking communities of Wapping or Canning Town now reside: in Kent
perhaps, or in north Essex, where I once heard of a whole pier in Wapping that
was entirely devoted to blood oranges from Morocco.

Nowadays, the former docks are so quiet that the disgraced Tory politician
David Mellor can broadcast his Classic FM programme *Across the Threshold* straight
from his home in the old dockmaster's house at St Katharine's Dock. Céline could
get his mind round the most monstrous possibilities, but the thought that London's
docks might ever become as empty and eerily silent as that would surely have
astonished him. 'There'd been no one around! Wapping Alley! Just imagine!'

Step out of Wapping's ancient pub the Prospect of Whitby on a summer Sunday
nowadays, and you may well find dragon-boats racing along the length of the
Shadwell Basin, the last-built section of the London Dock system. A drummer
seated in the bow of each of these elongated canoes pounds out a regular beat
while twenty or so enthusiastic rowers paddle frantically, in vague conformity
with the suggested rhythm. It is an agreeable scene to come across: cosmopolitan
and far superior to the dereliction that reigned here for years after the closure of
the London Docks.

The first such dragon boats to be seen on the Thames were brought over from
Hong Kong in the late 1980s, but they are now made in such places as Richmond

and the Isle of Wight. Their most ardent advocates on the Thames are to be found among the team-builders of the new corporate mecca around Canary Wharf. Far from being survivals of the Chinese settlement for which Limehouse was once famous, these dragon boats represent a new kind of Docklands Chinoiserie.

I was inclined to notice this difference, having just talked with Michael Wan, the owner of 'Good Friends', a Chinese restaurant a little further east at the end of a nondescript modern terrace of shops in Salmon Lane, just north of Hawksmoor's vast church St Anne's, Limehouse. This restaurant dates back to 1954, and although Mr Wan can claim a list of famous patrons, it has to be said that some of them, including Bobby Moore and Frank Sinatra have sinced passed away. The architects of the breakaway Social Democratic Party are said to have met here in the early eighties, too, under the auspices of David Owen, who moved to Limehouse in the first wave of gentrification. The food may still be worth travelling for, but Good Friends makes no concessions to recent trends in designer décor or life-style marketing, and it had its heyday in the sixties and seventies.

Mr Wan remarked that many Chinese people still live in the area, including some old men whose memories extend back to the 1920s, but the old nineteenth-century community, which, as Mr Wan chuckles, was started by Chinese sailors jumping ship,

Chinese East London in 1911.

has hardly left any residues at all. A few street names survive, such as the nearby Canton Street and Pennyfields, but the area was devastated by bombing in the Second World War, and later replaced by council estates. The obliteration has been such that Mr Wan has little choice but to refer enquirers on to the East London Cemetery, where many Chinese graves are still to be found.

A literary record remains, too, but it is one that was produced by onlookers rather than from within the Chinese settlement itself. The old dockside society of

East London certainly had problems of its own, but it was also fated to support a whole nation's idea of degeneracy. Social reformers did what they could, but, throughout the nineteenth century, East London was portrayed as a horror show whose monsters were in a league of their own – from John Williams, the seaman who committed the seven brutal Ratcliffe Highway murders in 1811 (using a shipyard maul among other weapons), to Jack the Ripper, and that emblem of proletarian monstrosity, the Elephant Man.

Concerned investigators came here to document alarming lapses in the 'Condition of England', but other witnesses only found a thrilling *frisson* in the disconnected and brutalized lives of those whom Jack London called 'People of the Abyss'. Thanks to the docks, thoroughbred patriots in the shires could imagine East London as a city of hideous fecundity, where brutes lurked in the fog. Hybrid, outcast and extreme, the East London riverside became an outdoor theatre in which visitors could dramatize their own worst fears.

Oriental Limehouse was an inspiration both to Charles Dickens, who opens his last novel, *The Mystery of Edwin Drood*, in a dishevelled opium den just off the Ratcliffe Highway; and to Sir Arthur Conan Doyle, who sent Sherlock Holmes out this way on several occasions. The Chinese themselves may have been busy setting up laundries and transferring restaurants to Soho, but their early twentieth-century chroniclers preferred to linger in the dockside opium den:

> Low couches lay around the walls and strange men decorated them: Chinese, Japs, Malays, Lascars, with one or two white girls; and sleek noiseless attendants swam from couch to couch… On one of the lounges a scorbutic nigger sat with a Jewess from Shadwell. The atmosphere churned. The dirt of years, tobacco of many growings, opium, betel nut, and moist flesh allied themselves in one grand assault on the nostrils.

That is how Chinese Limehouse was once described by Thomas Burke, a poet and journalist of the early twentieth century. Burke had his upriver visions of England: his anthology, *The Charm of England*, included more than enough poems in which 'sweet Thames' flowed on through the deep and reedy continuities of the home counties. But he was more at home in Wapping and Limehouse, where 'the acrid tang of the East hung on every breath of air', and where 'a bit of the Orient' could be found 'squatting at the portals of the west'.

In 'The Song Book of Quong Lee', Burke offered the lyrics of an imaginary Chinese poet much given to gazing out from 'the commanding and palatial Home for Asiatics' and spinning lines like 'There are no flowers in West India Dock Road'.[8] Writing as Quong Lee, Burke imagined lovely white girls in tenements by the Limehouse Causeway, combing their golden curls as they gaze out over a dockland hell in which 'cesspools of mud' loom large, along with mounds of refuse and offal.

Burke was generally a sympathetic observer who went out of his way to differentiate 'The Real East End' from the sink of depravity that 'the rest of England', with its 'fat, satin'd Bayswater wrath', took this small, hard-pressed stretch of London to be.[9] Yet in his short stories Burke unleashed his own appetite for Limehouse Gothic. In 'The Cane', for example, a young male teacher at a dockside school develops an addiction for thrashing 'a big girl of 13' called Dolly Uptrot.[10] Alarmed to find himself so aroused during these disciplinary sessions, he eventually breaks his cane, goes to the quayside and hurls himself into the river. Burke's story 'The Chink and the Child' features a beautiful, barely pubescent white girl, Lucy Burrows, an innocent piece of Thames whitebait who spends too much time hanging naked from the rafters while her father, a brutal and drunken boxer who embodies 'a curious mixture of athleticism and degeneracy', assaults her with a dog-whip. Lucy is eventually rescued by 'Chinky', who introduces her to the oriental ways of love. A sense of doom hangs heavy throughout, one that was splendidly captured by Lillian Gish, when she played Lucy Burrows in D. W. Griffiths's 1919 film of the story, *Broken Blossoms*.

A leafy pastorale upstream; brutality, drugs, exotic interbreeding downstream. That was the shape of the Thames not just for Thomas Burke, but also for Sax Rohmer, whose Chinese 'devil doctor' Fu Manchu presided over conspiracies that spread out along the Thames like a waterborne infection: 'Fu-Manchu's activities centred always about the London river. Undoubtedly it was his highway, his line of communication, along which he moved his mysterious forces. The opium den off Shadwell Highway; the mansion upstream…now the hulk lying off the marshes. Always he made his headquarters upon the river.'[11]

Fu Manchu's Limehouse den, 'a place of 'perfumed, slumberous darkness', surrounded by the 'smoke-laden vapours of the Lower Thames', may have borne little connection to the reality of Chinese Limehouse, but it certainly anticipated the loft-living scenario of our time. Indeed, that insulated warehouse's interior with its 'incensed stillness' is like an early anticipation of the show-apartment I visited at Aberdeen Wharf.

Noted in 1997 as one of the few 'unrestored' warehouses on Wapping High Street, this mid-nineteenth century warehouse has since been taken in hand by 'London Town plc' and made over into 'a Classic Riverfront Warehouse Conversion' of seventeen apartments organized around a glass-roofed atrium and targeted at 'interesting and sophisticated homeowners' of the kind who have already colonized this most sought-after of London's residential neighbourhoods.

Loft-living in this part of London may have been pioneered by artists and Bohemians, some of whom still hang on to their scruffy, experimental and perhaps occasionally even opiated spaces in early conversions such as Metropolitan Wharf just down the road. But the market has changed utterly since then. When I passed through, the building was full of prospective purchasers ready to pay the price of half a street in Yorkshire for a tight two-bedroom flat with a riverside view, but only enough underground parking space for a single Porsche.

LOOKING UPSTREAM FROM THE JEWISH EAST END

> *Time was, when the ships used to dock by Tower Bridge, and the immigrants into England could disappear without further ado among the streets and courts of the East End, there to begin life afresh. But all that had changed. Now, a permit was required from the Home Office.*
>
> Roland Camberton, *Rain on the Pavements* (1951)

Chinese Limehouse may have lost its image to more or less exploitative observers, but the literature of the Jewish East End was self-produced, a largely forgotten writing in which art is mixed up with prophecy, politics and protest, and in which fiction keeps breaking into raw testimony.

A number of considerable artists emerged from Jewish Whitechapel in the early decades of the twentieth century: Isaac Rosenberg, perhaps the greatest of the British poets of the Great War, the artist David Bomberg, and also the poet, translator and publisher John Rodker. There was something of a boom in the thirties, when writers from this world came into contact with Bohemian circles in Soho and elsewhere. There's not much to be said for the crude socialist realism of Simon Blumenfeld's *Jew Boy*; but there were also more accomplished writers such as Willie Goldman, whose autobiography, *East End My Cradle*, tells of growing up on a street awkwardly poised between Jewish Whitechapel and Gentile Wapping, and whose *The Light in the Dust* includes some splendidly acid portrayals of mainstream Bohemian circles in Hampstead.

The typical East End Jewish writer's career was a fractured and discontinuous thing; yet some saw it through, and few more impressively than Emanuel Litvinoff. 'There has always been a parochialism about English writing,' he once told me, explaining that the Jewish East End in which he grew up demanded a broader outlook.[12]

Litvinoff's parents had sailed into London in 1913, in the last years of Jewish emigration from the Russian Empire. Like many of the Jewish immigrants who had preceded them, travelling 'steerage' in what might as well have been cattle boats, they had hoped to reach America. But though the ship's captain may have taken their money for that journey he then dumped them in London, where they found themselves late-comers to a Whitechapel ghetto that was already densely populated by Russo-Polish Jews who had fled persecution in the Russian Empire – an emigration that became a terrified mass exodus in the early 1880s, thanks to the brutalities licensed by Tsar Alexander III.

Emanuel only remembers his father as a picture on a vanished wall in a long since demolished tenement building near Brick Lane. He was apparently a low-grade sweat-shop worker who thought of himself as an intellectual. Politically, he was an anarchist, who had probably been involved in student activity in Odessa. He went back to Russia during the Great War, obliged, like other male 'aliens' in Whitechapel, to choose between serving there or joining the British army on the

Western Front, but he got caught up in the Russian Revolution and never made it
back to London.

Litvinoff remembers Jewish Whitechapel as 'a small planet' – a place which was
at once miniature and epic in scale: a square mile into which a vast twentieth-
century history had been squeezed, and where 'people spoke of Warsaw, Kishinev,
Kiev, Kharkov, Odessa as if they were neighbouring suburbs'. If Whitechapel gave
Litvinoff a day-to-day awareness of distant historical convulsions, it also
bequeathed him abiding themes that would outlive the ghetto in which they were

found: his sympathy for victims of all kinds, and his concern
with 'not politics *per se*, but a kind of morality that is often
expressed in politics… You couldn't grow up in the Jewish
East End without having also lived inside the necessity of that
morality.' Unlike the figures of more conventional English
fiction, Litvinoff's characters crackle with the 'neurotic
tension' of those who feel alien wherever they are. His
Europe is seen from the quayside and prison cell: it has more
frontiers than reassuring landscapes, and its cities are known
less by their stately monuments than by shabby cafés in which
'all the world's foreigners' gather.

Whitechapel lived on in Litvinoff's mind, not just as an
evocative lost world, but as an abrasive insistence on
inconvenient truths and awkward questions. Yet, for a
while at least, he prospered. The film rights to his first
novel *The Lost Europeans* were sold even if the film, which
was to have starred Dirk Bogarde, never got made; and for
a time home was a six-bedroomed house in Abbots
Langley, Hertfordshire, with a Swiss maid and a Ford convertible in the drive.
In the late sixties, Litvinoff told the Zionists at a symposium in Tel Aviv that he
was content to live among generally 'mild, tolerant English people' in 'an
urbanized English village' where he was 'not conscious of segregation from my
neighbours'. But his second novel *The Man Next Door*, in which he did address
himself to English country life of the upriver variety, was hardly calculated to
please those neighbours.

**Canary Wharf soaring
upwards in 1990,
unhindered by those
critics who called it
'a monument in a
marsh'.**

Countless English writers may have feasted on the perceived degeneracy of the dockside East End, but this novel looks the other way. It concerns a Jewish family who, having made good in the Whitechapel lingerie trade (their firm is called 'Alluriste Ltd'), move into 'Maidenford', a village that would have been quite charming were it not for a vast sausage factory which fills the air with the repulsive and heavily symbolic stench of pork-production. The arriving newcomers are watched by their neighbour, Harold Bollam, a middle-aged and all but redundant vacuum-cleaner salesman. Bollam is a pastoralist of the racist kind, an English Thoroughbred for whom the sight of 'pure countryside' communicates 'a deeply religious feeling as if you'd been cleansed through and through', and he greets his new neighbours with a campaign of violence that escalates through arson to murder.

An author of resolutely downriver sympathies, Litvinoff initiates this horrible chain of events with an attempted rape, and it wasn't by accident that he placed it on the banks of the upstream Thames, a mile or so above Hampton Court.

THE MILLENNIUM – PAST AND PRESENT

It was thanks to the London Docklands Development Corporation (LDDC) that the Isle of Dogs woke up after many years of political neglect to find itself designated an Enterprise Zone in 1982. Not long afterwards, East Londoners could look on in amazement as Olympia and York's Canary Wharf rose steadily into the sky, bright blue in the early days, thanks to the protective sheeting in which its stainless steel panelling was clad during construction. Margaret Thatcher launched her 1987 election campaign here, undeterred by Prince Charles who, in that same year, wondered if Cesar Pelli's tower had to be quite so high.

Opinion in East London was more sharply divided. Many people, including some of the district's proverbial taxi drivers, marvelled at the sight, astonished by the engineering and by the very thought that 'Britain's first skyscraper' (Cesar Pelli's claim) could ever be made to stand on the watery site of the old West India Dock. I was among others, living in the area, who tried to suppress such wonder as they, too, might have felt at the technology of this unlikely development, insisting instead that Canary Wharf was a dubious American implant: a totalitarian obelisk, as we called it; the focal point of an inward-looking bastion of new wealth that would be sealed off against the poverty around it.

For David Widgery, a socialist doctor who worked in Limehouse throughout those years when 'you could put up an office block in E14 more easily than a garage extension in Henley', the LDDC was a 'secretive engine of corruption, a government-financed estate agent which has done to the Docklands what the Highland Clearances did to the north of Scotland'.[13]

The existing inhabitants of the Isle of Dogs were certainly well aware of the LDDC's lack of attention to the public infrastructure, whether it be roads, schools, or social housing. Indeed, the longer you had lived there, the more disorientated you were likely to feel as the development went ahead – and not surprisingly, since the LDDC was so keen to dissociate new Docklands from the old that they changed many of the traditional street names. The activists who had once declared the Isle of Dogs independent in protest against government policy for the area were now left struggling to make a community park out of the place where the dredgings from the West India Dock had customarily been dumped. It was a battle to keep even that discarded mud in place, since the Port of London Authority, which had got well into its new stride as a property developer by that time, was even considering selling it to tulip growers in Holland.

The LDDC is now gone, its role taken over by English Partnerships. Yet, whether you are at the Isle of Dogs or the Royal Docks complex downstream at Woolwich, there can be no doubt that the whole territory has been redefined. The slump that drove Olympia and York into receivership in 1992 is a distant memory; indeed, in 1995 Canary Wharf was acquired by a consortium led by Paul Reichman, one of the former owners of Olympia and York. Even the City Airport, to begin with little more than a shiny shed and a runway perilously glued on to a bombed out strip of land between the Royal Albert Dock and the King George V Dock, has achieved an undeniable measure of reality since it was lampooned in Iain Sinclair's novel *Downriver*.

No longer a farce, then, but exactly what kind of redefinition has been visited on this stretch of the river? The official estimates claim that 20,532 jobs were lost in the docklands area between 1981 and 1990, while 41,421 were gained. Yet those two figures applied to almost completely different worlds. Peter Hall writes of a 'total transformation' of the local economy: one which recycled the area, taking it out of industrial and dock-based employment and rededicated it to 'informational sector jobs' lured downriver from the City.[14] Far from seeking to help the old industries in the area, the LDDC is said to have run its own war against noisy or dirty occupations which conflicted with the new image. Some of the early, more Bohemian pioneers may rather have enjoyed the *frisson* of unlikely co-existence, but rubbing up against the old poor was at best a temporary attraction for the lifestyle magazines.

Having won its assault on the Royal Docks, which did not finally close until

Millennium Mills on the Royal Victoria Dock – a future that came and went.

1981, the regeneration drive is now beginning to spread far down into the defunct estuary, under the new format launched in 1995 as 'Thames Gateway'. Local authorities work in conjunction with English Partnerships, and the results are already rising up – major retail developments like Bluewater near Dartford, and endless housing schemes in Essex and Kent.

The development agencies have never been distinguished by their sensitivity to the cultural significance of the river, but in recent years the London Rivers Association has been busy trying to hammer a new idea of 'liquid history' into the rhetoric of regeneration. This is partly an ecological vision of the river, but it also makes the case for 'meaning' and for 'unlocking' the river's identity. The LRA and its members warn against treating the river just as 'liquid land', or a convenient lane for corporate helicopters.[15] They insist that the river is not an obstacle to be embanked, bridged, confined or merely forgotten like 'the brown God' of T.S. Eliot's description; and oppose those who talk of minimizing the reach of the tide ('the concept of a "tideless" Thames is a negation of this richness: a drowning of the river's identity in a Venetian pastiche').

For the London Rivers Association, the river offers us a 'reawakening of the senses', and planning concepts like 'reinforcing the river's edge', 'scale' and 'massing' need to be challenged as likely to lead to an excessively 'homogenous river environment'. Those struggling to keep the traditional river industries going in the estuary may still be inclined to reel in contemptuous astonishment when

they hear that the London Rivers Association is running conferences with names like 'Rivers of Meaning' in which the Thames and its foreshore are defended as a potential 'blue belt' (i.e., a 'watery equivalent of the green belt'), a place of contemplation and memory as well as nature. This may not be the kind of consideration that normally compels the volume-house-builders, but it is exactly the sort of defence that the tidal river now needs.

The Millennium Dome – the triumph of public art.

And the Millennium Dome? Looking across the river from the Royal Docks, it is impossible to ignore this extraordinary structure rising up on the site of an old gas works at Greenwich. Stephen Bayley, briefly the creative director of this project, has insisted that the dome is really a piece of 'Labour camp' – a tent rather than a building, and a triumph of style over substance.[16] Better surely to recognize it as a vast work of public art, a £40 million question mark written in the Thames-side air by Lord Rogers of Riverside.

While the Millennium Dome may be more than a match for the average rock-throwing vandal, I was relieved to find that it still faces considerable deflationary pressure from across the river. There is an enormous old building on the old Royal Victoria Dock, a gaunt hulk with the name 'Millennium Mills' written across it in proud red letters. Destined for conversion to loft-living and restaurants, it is a vast flour mill, the only survivor of four that once stood on the Royal Victoria Dock.

On 8 June 1914, the company that then owned Millennium Mills, Messrs Vernon and Sons, placed a large advertisement in *The Times*. A drawing showed their busy plant as it appeared from the water, with a sailing barge and other vessels passing in front of it. The text then explained that Messrs Vernon and Sons' flour mill in the Port of London was matched by an equally considerable establishment in the Port of Liverpool: 'palatial is the word that best describes them'.

Sold only in cotton bags of varying weights, Vernon and Sons' 'Millennium Flour' was described as the best that the world could ever produce. The company boasted that it had won hundreds of gold medals, including, and most proudly, 'The Miller' Cup which had been awarded to Millennium Flour on the eve of the new century in 1899. Having been selected from 'the best wheats of the world' (for 'Messrs Vernon and Sons have the world's harvests at their command'), the grain was then submitted to a carefully designed industrial process: mechanically sifted with an air blast 'to separate dirt, chaff and broken grains', 'scrubbed with hot water', and then dried in one of Vernon and Sons' 'immense purifying plants'.

As a product aimed at the rising twentieth-century masses, Millennium Flour contained 'all the absorbable phosphates' in wheat, but was free of the husky and 'unabsorbable' ones. Vernon and Sons went out of their way to announce that their Millennium Flour was most popular of all in the mining districts, where it was known to make 'beautifully white bread'. No doubt much of it was used more locally to produce 'white-bread sandwiches' of the well-meant but ill-nourishing kind that David Widgery remembered being made by the weeping wives of those dying dockers he used to visit as a young doctor in Limehouse. The fortunes being poured into the Millennium Dome will ensure a grand spectacle, but history has planted a salutary warning across the water: Millennium Mills, proof that the future does not always turn out to be good for your health.

ACKNOWLEDGEMENTS

This book was written to accompany a BBC 2 television series, so my initial debt is to the series producer and director James Runcie, and to the directors Nicky Pattison and Adam Low. I am also grateful to Gaby Hornsby and David Mackay, who worked as researchers on the four programmes, and to Lareine Shea, the production manager. My thanks to Kim Evans, who initiated the whole project, and also to Keith Alexander, the executive producer.

Special thanks are due to Tino Tedaldi who went way beyond the call of duty in providing so many of the photographs in this book, and to Anna Ottewill, Barbara Nash, Martha Caute, John Calvert and Susannah Parker at BBC Worldwide, who were patient and happy to live without too many swans and barges.

For various clues and suggestions, I am grateful to Anthony Barnett, Heinrich von Berenberg, D. G. Bond, Paul Gilroy, Claire Harman, Iain Sinclair, Sandy Nairne, Rose Jaijee, Patrick Keiller, Jamie Muir, Colin Ward and Simon Wright. Over the length of the river, I have been greatly assisted by diverse local historians and librarians. Special thanks are due to P. M. Delaney of the Wargrave Local History Society and Richard Willams, who helped considerably at Runnymede, as did the National Trust, in providing access to their archives. My grasp of Essex owes a lot to Jonathan Catton and Terry Carney of Thurrock Museum in Grays, and also to Annette Reeves of Thurrock Borough Council.

PW

PICTURE CREDITS

REFERENCES

PART ONE

1 Frank R. Turner & Will Stewart, *The Maunsell Sea Fort; Part Three: The World War Two Thames Estuary Defenders, the Human Element* (F. Turner, 1996), p. 128.
2 F.R. Turner, *The Sealand Story* (F. Turner, 1998), p. 14.
3 Steve Boggan, 'Global fraudsters use sea fortress as passport to riches', *The Independent*, 23.9.97.
4 First published in a West German magazine, Uwe Johnson's, 'Ein Schiff' was reprinted in G. Busch (ed), *Stichtworte zur 'Geistigen Situation der Zeit', 2. Band: Politik und Kultur* (Suhrkamp Verlag, 1979), pp. 799–814. A somewhat truncated English translation appeared as 'An Unfathomable Ship' in *Granta*, 6, 1982, pp. 261–76. See also F.R. Turner's pamphlet, 'The Wreck of the *USS Richard Montgomery*; the Thames Estuary Timebomb' (Turner, 1995).
5 Gerald Newman, *The Rise of English Nationalism; A Cultural History 1740–1830* (Weidenfeld & Nicolson, 1987), pp. 63–4.
6 Ebenezer Forrest's account of the peregrination is quoted from Charles Mitchell (ed.), *Hogarth's Peregrination* (Oxford University Press, 1952) pp. 7–9.
7 M.J. Dobson, 'Malaria in England: A Geographical and Historical Perspective', *Parassitologia 36*, 1994, pp. 35–60.
8 Quoted in Basil E. Cracknell, *Portrait of London River; the Tidal Thames from Teddington to the Sea* (Robert Hale, 1968) p. 146.
9 For the Cliffe explosion of 1911, see Ray Munday, 'The Cliffe Explosion of 1911', *Bygone Kent*, Vol.15, No.1. Also coverage in *Chatham News*, 29 July 1911, p. 7.
10 Richard Church, *Kent* (Robert Hale, 1948) p. 236.
11 Charles Dickens, *Dickens's Dictionary of the Thames 1887; from its source to the Nore* (1888).
12 Suzanne Murphy, 'Pier we go', *Gravesend Reporter*, 15 October, 1998.
13 Conrad Dixon, 'Lascars: the forgotten seamen', in R. Ommer & G. Panting (eds.), *Working men who got wet* (Newfoundland, 1980), pp. 265–77.
14 Canon S. Gummer and J. S. Gummer, *When the Coloured People Come* (Oldbourne, 1966).
15 Charles Dickens, 'The Long Voyage' in *American Notes and Reprinted Pieces*, (Chapman and Hall), pp. 154–8.
16 George Orwell, *Down and Out in Paris and London* (1933), (Penguin, 1966), p. 113.

PART TWO

1 See Glyn H. Morgan, *Forgotten Thameside* (Thames Bank Publishing Co., 1951), p. 160.
2 This account of the Bata story is based on Anthony Cekota, *Entepreneur Extraordinary; The Biography of Tomas Bata* (University Press of the International University of Social Studies, 1968) and Anthony Cekota, *The Stormy Years of an Extaordinary Enterprise; Bata 1932–1945* (University Sokol Publications, 1985). I have also drawn on Thomas J. Bata, *Bata; Shoemaker to the World* (Stoddart, 1990) and copies of the *Bata Record* and other company papers held at the Thurrock Museum in Grays.
3 Vladimir Karfik, 'Bata Architecture in Zlin,' reprinted from the catalogue of an exhibition called *Bata Architektura a Urbanismus 1910–1950*, held at Zlin in 1991, p. 106.
4 Glyn H. Morgan, *op. cit.*, p. 12.
5 Basil E. Cracknell, *Canvey Island; The History of a Marshland Community* (University of Leicester, 1959), p. 23.
6 For Canvey as a Plotland Arcadia, see Dennis Hardy and Colin Ward, *Arcadia for All; the Legacy of a Makeshift Landscape* (Mansell, 1984).

7 Quoted in David Matless, *Landscape and Englishness* (Reaktion, 1998), p. 42.
8 Buchanan's novel *Andromeda*, is quoted by Cracknell, p. 39.
9 Hilda Grieve, *The Great Tide* (County Council of Essex, 1959), p. 855.
10 L.T.C. Rolt, *The Thames from Source to Mouth* (Batsford, 1951), p. 7.
11 William J. Fishman, *East End 1888* (Duckworth, 1988), p. 12.
12 A.B. Bryant, quoted in William Kent, *John Burns, Labour's Lost Leader* (Williams & Norgate, 1950) p. 38.
13 Ben Tillett, *Memories and Reflections* (1931), quoted in Kent, pp. 42–3.
14 Jack Lindsay, *Rising Tide* (Bodley Head, 1953), p. 269.
15 Jack Dash, *Good Morning Brothers!* (Lawrence & Wishart, 1969).
16 Joseph Addison, *The Spectator*, 20 May 1712.
17 Samuel Smiles, *Lives of the Engineers*, Vol.1 (1862), (David & Charles, 1966), pp. 2–16. On Captain Perry and the Dagenham Breach see pp. 69–82. Also L.T.C. Rolt, *The Thames from Mouth to Source* (Batsford, 1951), p. 5.
18 Daniel Defoe, *A Tour Through the Whole Island of Great Britain*, Vol.1 (Everyman, 1962), p. 9.

PART THREE

1 Michael Drayton 'Rowland's Song in Praise of Fairest Beta' in John Nichols, *Progresses, Public Processions of Queen Elizabeth* (1823), Vol.3, p. 63.
2 Alan Jenkins, *The Book of the Thames* (Macmillan, 1983), p. 13.
3 See W. H. Herendeen, *From Landscape to Literature: The River and the Myth of Geography* (Pittsburgh, 1986). See also Simon Schama, *Landscape and Memory* (HarperCollins, 1995).
4 M. Prichard and H. Carpenter, *A Thames Companion* (Oxford University Press, 1981).
5 Fred S. Thacker, *The Stripling Thames* (Thacker, 1909) p. 354.
6 Mr & Mrs. S.C. Hall, *The Book of*

the Thames from its Rise to its Fall
(London, 1859), p. 14.
7 Arthur Williams, *Round About the
Upper Thames* (Duckworth, 1922).
8 J.R.L. Anderson, *The Upper Thames*
(Eyre & Spottiswoode, 1970), p. 71.
9 Ernest Rhys (ed.), *The Old Country:
A Book of Love and Praise in England*
(Dent, 1917).
10 Eric de Maré, *Time on the Thames*
(Harvester Press, 1975), p. 233.
11 E. P. Thompson, *William Morris,
Romantic to Revolutionary* (Pantheon,
1975), p. 513.
12 May Morris, *William Morris; Artist,
Writer, Socialist* (Oxford, 1936), p. 36.
13 See Eugene D. Lemire, *The
Unpublished Lectures of William Morris*
(Wayne State University Press,
1969), p. 217.
14 Fermin Rocker, *The East End Years;
A Stepney Childhood* (Freedom Press,
1998), p. 58.
15 A Crawford, *C.R. Ashbee; Architect,
Designer and Romantic Socialist* (Yale
University Press, 1985), p. 13.
16 Paul Hirst, *Associative Democracy*,
(Polity Press, 1994), p. 103.
17 Meredith Veldman, *Fantasy, the
Bomb, and the Greening of Britain:
Romantic protest, 1945–80* (Cambridge
University Press, 1994), p. 38.
18 See Martin Adeney, *Nuffield; a
Biography* (Robert Hale, 1993). Also
F.J. Minns (ed.), *Wealth Well-Given;
the Enterprise and Benevolence of Lord
Nuffield* (Alan Sutton, 1994).
19 Paul Nash, *Outline* (1949), p. 122.
See also Roger Cardinal, *The
Landscape Vision of Paul Nash*
(Reaktion, 1989).
20 J.R.L. Anderson, *op. cit.*, p. 26.

PART FOUR

1 See Patricia Burstall, *The Golden
Age of the Thames* (David & Charles,
1981).
2 T.H. White, *The Age of Scandal;
An Excursion through a Minor Period*
(Jonathan Cape, 1950), p. 216.
3 This is the apocryphal account of
Wargrave-born 'Tom Perkins' as

recorded in Alan Wykes, *An Eye on the
Thames* (Jarrolds, 1966), pp. 164–6.
4 Quoted in Dora Perez-Tibi, *Dufy*
(Thames & Hudson, 1989), p. 315.
5 A. E. Hobbs, *Trout of the Thames*
(Herbert Jenkins Ltd.), p. 66.
6 Graham Robertson, quoted in
Peter Haining (ed.), *Paths to the River
Bank* (Souvenir, 1983), p. 13.
7 Robert de Board, *Counselling for
Toads; a Psychological Adventure*
(Routledge, 1998).
8 See Richard Williams, *Runnymede;
a Pictorial History* (Egham-by-
Runnymede Historical Society,
1995).
9 Quoted in Bill Schwarz, 'Politics
and Rhetoric in the Age of Mass
Culture', *History Workshop Journal*,
46, 1998, pp. 141–2.
10 Charles Chaplin, *My Autobiography*
(Bodley Head, 1964, p. 140).
11 Norman Shrapnel, *A View of the
Thames* (Collins, 1977), p. 34.

PART FIVE

1 Rufus Noel-Buxton gives his own
account of this escapade in *Westminster
Wader* (Faber & Faber, 1957). See also
his article 'A Ford at Westminster'
(*The Observer,* 30 March 1952) and
his poem 'The Ford' (Caravel Press,
1955).
2 Tom Nairn, 'Palace of
Enchantments', *New Statesman*,
11 November 1988.
3 Macaulay's image, quoted in Noel-
Buxton's *Westminster Wader*, dates
from 1840. It occurs in a passage
concerned to demonstrate the
enduring power of the Roman
Catholic Church, which Macaulay
imagined would outlast the ruin of
London. See T. Döring, 'Discovering
the Mother Country', *Journal for the
Study of British Cultures*, Vol. 4/1–2
(Tübingen, 1997), pp. 181–201.
4 Evelyn Waugh, 'Awake my Soul! It
is a Lord', *The Spectator*, 8 July 1955.
5 Robert Byron, *Imperial Pilgrimage*
(London Transport, 1937) p. 31.
6 J. H. Meister, quoted in Leon

Radzinowicz, *A History of English
Criminal Law and its Administration from
1750, Vol. 2, The Clash between Private
Initiative and Public Interest in the
Enforcement of the Law* (Stevens, 1956),
p. 349. For another description of the
eighteenth-century river Sir Joseph
G. Broodbank's 2-volume *History of
the Port of London* (1921). Also
Stephen Inwood, *A History of London*
(Macmillan, 1998), pp. 317–24. And
Elizabeth Williamson and Nikolaus
Pevsner, *London Docklands; an
Architectural Guide* (Penguin, 1998).
7 Colquhoun, Patrick, *A Treatise on the
Police of the Metropolis, explaining the
various crimes and misdemeanours which
at present are felt as a pressure upon the
Community; and suggesting remedies for
their prevention* (C. Dilly, 1796).
8 Thomas Burke, *The Song Book of
Quong Lee* (Allen & Unwin) 1920.
9 See Thomas Burke, *The Real East
End* (Constable, 1932). The Bayswater
remark is quoted from his *Limehouse
Nights; Tales of Chinatown* (Grant
Richards, 1917), p. 113.
10 Thomas Burke, 'The Cane' in
Whispering Windows (1921).
11 Sax Rohmer, *The Book of Fu
Manchu* (St Albans Press, 1930),
p. 186.
12 For Emanuel Litvinoff's own
portrait of Whitechapel see *Journey
Through a Small Planet* (Michael
Joseph, 1972). For his account of
growing up in and leaving
Whitechapel see 'A Jew in England'
(*Jewish Quarterly*, Spring 1967).
13 David Widgery, *Some Lives! A GP's
East End* (Sinclair Stevenson, 1991),
p. 215.
14 See the chapter called 'The City of
Capitalism Rampant' in Peter Hall's
Cities in Civilization (Weidenfeld &
Nicolson, 1998), pp. 888–931.
15 London Rivers Association, *Rivers
of Meaning; Getting in Touch with the
Thames* (London Rivers Association,
1996).
16 Stephen Bayley, *Labour Camp; The
Failure of Style over Substance* (Batsford,
1998).

INDEX